Hitchhiking to Kathmandu

MY OVERLAND ODYSSEY, 1974

KAREN SOLOMON

Hitchhiking to Kathmandu:
MY OVERLAND ODYSSEY, 1974
BY KAREN SOLOMON

© Copyright 2018 by Karen Solomon. All rights reserved.

Copy Editing:
Kate Lemberg

Original Cover Art Direction:
Violette Larsen

Cover and Interior Design & Layout:
Brett Burner
Lamp Post Printing & Publishing Consultants

Without limiting the rights under copyright reserved above, no part of this publication – whether in printed or ebook format, or any other published derivation – may be reproduced, stored in or introduced into a retrieval system, or transmitted, in any form or by any means (electronic, mechanical, photocopying, recording or otherwise), without the prior written permission of the publisher. This includes review or public release by any form of media, social media, news source, or informational publication.

The scanning, uploading, and distribution of this book via the Internet or via any other means without the permission of the publisher is illegal and punishable by law. Please purchase only authorized electronic or print editions and do not participate in or encourage electronic piracy of copyrightable materials.

ISBN-13: 978-1-60039-077-7

Published by Karen Solomon

CONTENTS

Preface xi

Chapter One: **Leaving Home** | *Germany, Austria, Greece* 1

Chapter Two: **The Gateway to the East** | *Istanbul, Turkey* 6

Chapter Three: **Halloween in Herat** | *Afghanistan* 11

Chapter Four: **Welcome to India** | *Delhi and Benares (Varanasi)* 23

Chapter Five: **Thanksgiving in Kathmandu** | *Kathmandu* 30

Chapter Six: **Our First Trek!** | *Helambu/Langtang Region of Nepal* 40

Chapter Seven: **Hanging Out at the Monkey Temple** | *Kathmandu* 45

Chapter Eight: **Happy New Year 1975!** | *Pokhara, Nepal* 58

Chapter Nine: **A Land of Contrasts** | *Agra and the Taj Mahal* 66

Chapter Ten: **Bombay and My New Journal!** | *Bombay* 72

Chapter Eleven: **Are We Still in India?** | *Goa* 79

Chapter Twelve: **Indian Hospitality is the Best!** | *Bombay* 102

Chapter Thirteen: **Dropping in with the Locals** | *Kathmandu* 125

Chapter Fourteen: **My Birthday in Ghoripani on the Jomsom Trek** | *Pokhara* 139

Chapter Fifteen: **It's Hard to Say Goodbyes** | *Kathmandu* 159

Chapter Sixteen: **A Grand Finale at a Five Star Hotel!** | *Delhi* 170

Chapter Seventeen: **Home to Belmont** | *Europe* 177

Epilogue 193

Happy 90th Birthday, Dad!

Better late than never! It only took forty-three years to get this book done. Thanks for being the coolest Dad anyone could imagine, and for the foresight in handing me that shoe box filled with the seventy-six letters which made this book possible.

ACKNOWLEDGMENTS

This book is dedicated to my extraordinary parents, Paul and Jackie Solomon, who for the duration of my eight plus months journey stayed in touch and wondered if they'd see their eldest daughter again. Their love and support has always provided the foundation for my incredible life.

Mom, I'm sorry you died so young, I miss you.

To my wonderful stepmom Phyl Solomon, whose marriage to Dad continues to inspire the entire Significant Crew as we make our way in the world. You're the best, and I am deeply grateful for how happy you've made Dad, and for you both continuing to provide a home base for me on the East Coast. I'm so lucky to have such amazing parents still holding a foundation for me as I am now in my seventh decade.

To my "baby" sister Jeri Solomon whose steadfast love and successful entrepreneurship never ceases to amaze and motivate me. Can't imagine a better sister!

I'd be hugely remiss if I didn't acknowledge my journey partner, David Kaloustian, without whose invitation I might never have gotten to Nepal, and certainly wouldn't have had this entire life changing experience. I am grateful for his friendly, easy going manner and ability to tap into humor and diplomacy in order to find solutions even in some of the most challenging situations. Thanks for taking such good care of me on our journey, Dave!

Additionally, there's no describing the feeling of connection, love and support I experienced upon reaching a foreign city to find letters awaiting me from friends and family. You all kept me going through times of unbearable homesickness. Special thanks to my sister Debra Solomon, to my Grammy Esther Solomon, my Aunt Shaari Mittel, Aunt Eleanor and Uncle Hank Henkoff as well as Linda Krause and my other high school friends for keeping in touch throughout my journey.

PREFACE

The first fourteen months of my life were spent in the back of a light blue 1957 VW Bug traveling around Europe with Mom and Dad. We lived in a trailer on an air force base in Verdun, France where Dad was a flight surgeon in the US Air Force, luckily during peaceful times. Dad took out the back seat to make a playpen for me and I've heard stories of the many times they almost lost their wild and curious little toddler as I reached for interesting things floating in the canals of Venice or chased the pigeons in St. Mark's Square. It's no wonder they had me wear a harness!

We returned to Dad and Mom's home town of Boston, Massachusetts so Dad could do his pediatric residency. We lived in Cambridge for those early years. During my kindergarten year, we moved to Belmont, a suburb just west of Boston so Dad could set up his practice. I lived in Belmont with my family including my sister Deb, two years younger than me, and our younger sister Jeri born when I was in the fourth grade, until my high school graduation in 1974.

At the age of 13, my family and I visited a relative who lived in Mexico City. This was my first exposure to developing countries and the huge disparity between rich and poor was first made evident to me. My heart hurt to see hungry children with outstretched hands. Dad reminds me that I asked for my next two years of allowance to give to those kids.

My first big solo venture away from home and family was during the summer of 1972 when I was sixteen. I had just completed my sophomore year of high school, and was quite miserable, feeling lost and rather alienated, not a part of any one social group that had any redeeming qualities. Instead, I was involved with a rough bunch of kids which worried my parents. When a camp counseling job fell through at the last minute, my parents decided that it'd be best to get me out of town and I agreed. Next thing I knew, I found myself spending a summer in Israel, working on a kibbutz and traveling around the country with a group of fellow 16 and 17 year olds.

That was a pivotal trip during which I got in touch with my (secular) Judaism as well as other essential aspects of myself that had been obscured through the haze of peer pressure and pot smoking. Upon my return home I felt a new sense of confidence and clarity that the public school I'd been attending was not the right place for me. After a search of private schools in the Boston area, I was lucky enough to join the senior class at The Palfrey Street School in Watertown, Massachusetts.

It was Columbus Day weekend, 1973, when I found myself in the woods of Southern Vermont with 50 other teens and young twenty-somethings. Together we pitched tents on land owned by a friend of Ned Ryerson, the headmaster of the Palfrey Street School. Never having been camping, I was delighted by the Woodstock-like scene.

Food was prepared and shared, joints and gallon jugs of half milk/half Kahlua were passed around the campfire. After a while people pulled out guitars, harmonicas, a fiddle, coolers for percussion, even spoons joined in the impromptu musical jam.

At one point a cute guy sitting across from me started playing his flute. This prompted a boy next to me to say, "When I'm good and drunk I'll take out my flute…" It turned out he was a beginner, having had only two lessons. I'd started playing flute in 4th grade, but had quit when I didn't think it was "cool" to play classical music and march with the high school band. But sitting there amongst all those musicians playing hip rock and roll music inspired me to borrow his flute. Blessed with the gift of a musical ear inherited from Dad, I found myself easily playing leads, harmonies, etc. I was delighted to participate in my first jam session.

Next thing I knew, I'd fallen in love with David, that cute flute player across the campfire. We subsequently became inseparable throughout the rest of my senior year.

Just a few days prior to that fateful meeting, David had returned from a ten-month overland trip from Europe to Asia with his best high school friend Cedric. Most of that time had been spent trekking in Nepal. The only reason they returned home was because they'd run out of funds. Dave's goal was to get a job, accumulate a few thousand dollars, and head back to Nepal. Their stories, along with hundreds of great photos, inspired me to put Nepal on my ever-growing bucket list.

Dad had agreed to pay for "that hippie school" if I promised to attend an extra semester in order to make up for the academics he felt I'd lost while miserable at Belmont High School. Desperate to attend Palfrey, where I felt I'd be seen and understood, I had agreed to Dad's deal.

But come April of my senior year just as I was turning 18, Dave invited me to travel back to Nepal with him. I queried the school administration to determine if I had enough credits to graduate with my class in June. They assured me I more than qualified for a diploma. Thus I informed my parents that, rather than staying in high school that extra semester (seriously?) or going straight to college, as was expected for all the graduating seniors we knew, I'd be traveling to Nepal with Dave.

I'm sure you can imagine how well that went over. Like all educated middle class Jewish Americans in the '70s, my parents had every expectation for their intelligent daughter to go to college. Their daughter, however, had a much more irresistible offer, and quite a bit of money saved up from waitressing at The Pewter Pot Muffin House in Harvard Square after school and on weekends. As fate would have it, Massachusetts passed a law making the drinking age 18 a month prior to my 18th birthday. Upon turning 18, I immediately got myself a job serving cocktails at Charlie's Beef and Beer House in Somerville, MA. Squirreling away every penny I made, despite my parents' protests, plans were made for Dave and me to leave the United States in early October.

I was grateful that though Dad and Mom understandably opposed the trip, Dad did give Dave $50 for film and made sure I had the required inoculations and a decent first aid kit. The trip was worrisome enough without being concerned that I'd become ill!

On October 6, 1974, just six months after graduating with my high school class, Dave and I started what would become an eight-month and one week journey. Along with our external frame backpacks equipped with tent, sleeping bags, pads and a stove, we were driven to Montreal by Dave's dad, and off we flew to Munich. As we drove off from the home I'd known since kindergarten, I felt both terrified and excited. I will never forget the image of Dad and Mom standing outside the front door with arms raised in goodbyes, no doubt wondering when and if they'd see their eldest daughter again.

We landed at the tale end of Munich's wild and crazy Oktoberfest and got over our jet lag to the tune of giant steins of beer served by hearty and busty frauleins.

Eager to get to Nepal in order to trek before the dead of winter, we proceeded to hitchhike through the black forest into Austria, where an encounter with a former member of the SS completely freaked me out, prompting us to get the heck out of Austria at dawn the next day.

We then hitchhiked through the strangely dark police state known as Yugoslavia at that time. We were picked up by Harold, a kind German man in his twenties. We piled into his VW bug along with him and his tiny German shepherd puppy and found ourselves camping for a few days on Greece's Aegean Coast. We sampled ouzo and experienced a tremendous storm, which caused our tent to cave on us on the one night we didn't think we'd need to put up our rain fly. The rest of that soggy night was spent huddled together in Harold's car.

Whenever I could, I'd write letters home to friends and family or spend time capturing as many of the bewildering daily experiences I was having into my journal. After only two weeks, I was dismayed to realize I'd left the first journal of my trip in the back of a Greek taxi cab never to be seen again.

I started another journal in which I wrote every day from late October through January. That book came with me everywhere, and grew more and more valuable as it swelled with stories, along with the names and addresses of cool Westerners we met along our path. We talked of visiting them in their home countries of Switzerland, France, Italy, Australia, Brazil… plus many of the United States I'd yet to see. I picked flowers, which I'd press and eventually glue into my journal. Various memorabilia I'd collect along the way got included as well.

And so I found myself at just eighteen years of age halfway across the world from everything and everyone I knew and loved except for David, of course. At that time, international phone calls were astronomically expensive, and of course there was no internet. The only feasible way to communicate was by letter, which could take upwards of a month to six weeks to reach the States.

The blank pages in journals and letters provided a vehicle for me to capture and process the huge amount of stimulation coming at me from all directions. Given my days were filled with new and unfamiliar situations, sights, sounds, landscapes, and people speaking strange languages, wearing exotic clothing, eating weird food, practicing age-old customs that didn't make sense… Those journals were my lifeline and felt like my best friend providing a safe haven in which I could confide my deepest experiences with no fear of judgment.

After parting ways with Harold and the puppy, a Greek truck driver picked us up and drove us to Istanbul, where we reveled in the stunning grandeur of that ancient city known as the Gateway to the East. That's where everything started to change.

In Istanbul's iconic Pudding Shop, we ran into Kathy and Jeff, a couple from Ohio whom Dave and Cedric had met two years prior at the Mt. Everest Basecamp. Little did we know that the next two months would find us weaving in and out of one another's lives including a three-week trek together in Nepal's Helambu/Langtang region.

At the Pudding Shop we also met an American guy with a VW Camper van who was on his way to Afghanistan and was happy to take us as far as Kabul. Unbeknownst to us, he was en route to buy himself an Afghani woman. When my feminist self heard that, I let him know my thoughts, causing him to dramatically pull over in the middle of the desert in Iran demanding that we get out. Fortunately, Diplomatic Dave was able to convince him to take us as far as Tehran where we'd easily be able to find a bus to take us further East. Who knows what might have happened had we been let out in the desert! I like to think I learned a lesson about mouthing off without considering the consequences, though some may beg to differ.

Suffice to say we were off on a grand adventure. The next eight months would see us spending three weeks in Afghanistan, swiftly traveling over the Khyber Pass into Pakistan and then crossing into India at Amritsar, then on to New Delhi. Eager to reach Nepal prior to the bitter winter cold setting in, we stayed in Delhi just long enough to attain the required visas.

After a few glorious months spent trekking in the Helambu/Langtang region outside Kathmandu and exploring both Kathmandu and Pokhara, we were forced to leave the country due to the impending coronation for the King. I remember *International Time Magazine* stating something like: "In preparation for King Birendra's Coronation and the visiting dignitaries from over 60 countries coming to Kathmandu,

temples are being renovated, streets paved, stray dogs poisoned, and Western hippies, who for the last ten years have regarded Kathmandu as a kind of real-life Shangri-La, have been banished for the occasion."

Unable to extend our tourist visas, we traveled by bus and train down to Agra to see the Taj Mahal. Unable to afford first class train tickets, we'd been advised to always travel with reserved second-class seats. But since there was a two-week wait for reserved seats to Agra, and we were anxious to get there, I let Dave talk me into traveling unreserved amongst India's poorest people.

Most people who've been to India have at least one Indian train escapade to recount. In the 1970s, there were way fewer cars on the road, limiting transportation to scooters (some with as many as five family members riding at once), walking, bicycles, bicycle rickshaws, a few taxis, and of course the massive infrastructure that made up the Indian train system. All trains were filled to the brim with every manner of humanity ranging from wealthy women sporting brightly colored silk saris and dripping with gold to disfigured beggars in rags. The roof of most trains were piled high with luggage mixed with people, chickens and geese in bamboo cages, and an occasional goat tethered to whatever seemed most sturdy.

Anticipating our return to Nepal post-coronation, we had stored our heavy trekking and camping gear in Kathmandu in order to travel more lightly to India. Dave and I each were traveling with a fairly large duffel bag and an Army Navy surplus issued day-pack. We'd gotten onto a train in a city on the Indian side of the Nepalese border and managed to secure ourselves a spot in the in-between section of two cars as every single seat and bunk was overstuffed with poor locals. The rectangular space we found ourselves in was the width of the train by about six feet.

Preparing for the eight-hour journey, we found ourselves sitting on our duffel bags with our smaller packs on our laps, leaning against the wall of the compartment. To my left was a door to the outside that had a window in its top half. There was a nasty excuse for a bathroom diagonally across from us. It was literally a small room with a hole in the floor of the train where waste went straight to the tracks below. From the disgusting smell it seemed like most people had terrible aim…

Just as the train was pulling out of the station where we'd boarded, two larger-than-average Indian men in turbans forced their way through that open window and landed half on top of me. One of them moved a few feet away while the other stayed standing squished between me and the door. Along with the other fifty or sixty men in our small area, they spent the next few hours staring at the two of us, as we were the only Westerners dumb enough to be traveling without reservations.

Hardly an express train to Agra, the train would stop at stations unknown to us and people would get on and off, stepping on me as they clamored out the top half of the door. Just as I was beginning to relax with the thought that we'd be in Agra soon enough, the train slowed down, and the big guy next to me called to his friend who answered him loudly. When I turned my head to see if the other guy was about to step on me en route to the exit window, the first guy grabbed the pack off my lap and leapt off the still moving train. Naturally I screamed, causing Dave to take out his mighty Swiss Army Knife, and I remember the short blade gleaming as it reflected the dim light from the only naked light bulb in the compartment.

I admit it… I was completely freaked out. I was more than 7,000 miles from home and had just been robbed on an Indian train! Sobbing, I managed to tell Dave what had happened, and he stood up, dragging me and the rest of our luggage into that disgusting bathroom. There we stood holding our duffel bags against the wall for about another hour, tears streaming down my cheeks until we heard the conductor announce that we were coming into Lucknow, which is a substantial city where we assumed we'd find a safe place to stay.

As always, when we got off the train and entered the station, we were stormed by dozens of Indian men and boys offering us rides, hotels, etc. Pushing our way through the throngs, we made it to the street. There we found ourselves smack in the middle of a Sikh wedding with the bride and groom sitting atop a gaily decorated elephant. A beautifully dressed Sikh man who spoke decent English referred us to a hotel where we then splurged to the massive amount of $20, a huge leap from the $2-$6 we'd become accustomed to spending per night.

Once in the hotel room I realized that though my passport, money and traveler's checques were safe in the money belt stashed under my clothing, I'd lost the beloved journal in which I'd been writing since I'd left my first journal in the back of that Grecian cab months earlier. Three-and-a-half months of emotional outpouring were gone, as were the dozens of names and addresses of people we'd met from all over the world with every intention of staying in touch and visiting other foreign lands in the future. I was inconsolable.

The Taj Mahal was spectacular despite my dreary mood. We walked around and took photos while the hotel proprietors did our laundry for us. I unfortunately had managed to contract body lice, which lined the seams of my clothing, causing me to itch furiously. As the hotel staff washed my clothing in boiling water, I remember wearing Dave's corduroys.

I can't resist telling one more story that occurred in Agra, reminding us that we were "not in Kansas anymore, Toto…"

Unwilling to travel unreserved again, and eager to reach Bombay (Mumbai was still called Bombay in those days), where we'd been invited to stay with the family of some of Dad's patients, we decided to go to the train station in Agra and try our luck at having some train official feel sorry for us and thus give us the coveted reserved tickets that usually took the requisite two week wait.

So off we went. Upon arriving at the station, we decided to divide and conquer, meaning we'd see how persuasive each of us might be with different railroad officials.

I found myself engaged in a conversation with a guy who turned out to be the second-in-command official at that station, which was a very prestigious position. His head bobbed Indian style as he assured me there'd be no problem getting us last minute reservations; he felt badly that we'd had such a negative experience in his beloved country. He asked what I did in America, and I foolishly told him I was a cocktail waitress. At this point he became extremely interested, leaning forward saying, "No problem – tonight I will come to your hotel with 'the rum,' and you will serve it to your husband and me with coke." In exchange he promised to get us reservations on a train the next day. Back then it was illegal for Indian citizens to drink alcohol, and we tourists actually had alcohol stamped on our visas allowing us to drink in their country.

Though he was definitely a bit too excited about "the rum," I had no reason for concern, as Dave was with me and we were cleverly wearing fake wedding rings. It simply wasn't worth telling people we were "living in sin" as it was too outside their conceptual grasp.

Amused and delighted that we would be on our way in style the next day, we awaited the official's arrival at our hotel. We heard our proprietor greeting him, and we opened our door.

I remember every detail of that room like I was there a few days ago, rather than over 40 years ago. There was a bed, cracked blue cinder block walls, a bathroom, and a little writing desk with a chair in which I sat writing a letter (since I'd not yet replaced that journal). The official came in, sat on the bed, and opened up his sport jacket to reveal a brown bottle with no label, proudly indicating it was "the rum." He then ordered Dave to go out and get us some coke and three glasses. The moment Dave walked out of the room shutting the door behind him, the guy leaned over my desk, his face about six inches from mine, and said, "Please, one kiss." Aghast, I told him I was a married woman and how could he be so rude, to which he replied, head bobbing, "No matter. Do you want those tickets?"

Meanwhile I could hear jovial Dave talking up the hotel staff in his inimitable friendly manner, and I silently willed him to come back into our room to save me from this guy. After what seemed like a half hour (but was probably five minutes), Dave came back with the coke. As I stewed silently, we drank our rum and cokes while the two of them chatted. Eventually the train official went into the bathroom, at which point I was able to quickly let Dave know the guy had made a pass at me. On that note, Dave managed to end the evening rather swiftly. We were told to meet the guy the next day at the train station. He couldn't procure the reservations after all and would see what he might do the next day.

In typical Indian style, we found out that there was another lesser known train station in Agra where we were indeed able to get reserved seats the very next day. The fact that no one had offered us that alternative solution is simply one aspect of just how exasperating India can be.

After our Agra escapades we went on to Bombay where we stayed with the family of some of Dad's patients who lived in Boston. They revered "Dr. Paul" and treated Dave and me like royalty. Their home felt like an oasis after the many cheap hippie hotels we'd been staying in. I felt myself begin to recover from being robbed.

While in Bombay, I bought my third and final journal of the trip and started writing on February 1, 1975. Sadly I'd lost four months of travel journaling when my book was stolen.

I still consider this journal, along with the letters and photos from that trip, amongst my most prized possessions. They, and now this book, represent an invaluable time in my life that can't, nor shouldn't, be forgotten. It was quite the way to come of age in the '70s, and

I am struck by the fact that as far as I can tell, not one other teenager has published about their coming of age experience traveling from Munich to Kathmandu in the 1970s.

We spent time in Agra, Bombay, and Goa, where we lived on the beach for a few weeks with friends, then back to Bombay and eventually back to Nepal in April as planned. While sharing a house on the beach in Goa with friends from Georgia, I started feeling ill. It turned out that I had come down with Hepatitis A from drinking bad water during our trek in the Himalaya the previous December. I remember that fateful gulp of water I'd had in hopes of relieving the burning sensation caused by the ever present chilis in Nepalese food. Unfortunately the water was not yet purified. In those days we carried Halazone tablets that required at least 20 minutes to dissolve, and desperate to temper the fiery chilis, I couldn't wait.

Leaving Dave hanging out and partying at Colva Beach in Goa, I flew back to Bombay from Panjim, Goa's capital, and landed back at the home of Dad's patients. I begged them not to inform their family of my illness, as I knew Dad would be on the next plane to rescue me. Fortunately, they agreed, and my folks never knew I'd been sick until I arrived home.

The family took wonderful care of me, sending me to Dr. Desai with samples of my pee that I carried in a coke bottle every other day. It started out a quite frightening coca cola color, getting lighter each subsequent day. The doctor prescribed sugar cane juice with lime and ginger, roasted chickpeas, mandarin oranges, and buttermilk (which I detest and thus poured out the window for the stray dogs below).

After a few weeks of convalescing during which I relaxed into my stay with that lovely, hospitable Indian family, Dave came back from Goa in order for us to continue our travels back to Nepal.

While there Dave and I were asked to play our flutes at a Ghandhian school where one of the aunts taught. There we were confronted by about 400 girls all wearing white uniforms with purple sashes. Each wore a ring in her nose and her black hair braided and looped up like Princess Leia would make popular several years later.

After playing the Star Spangled Banner (upon request) and as many pop-rock songs we could think of, a 16-year-old girl named Archana approached me asking if I'd be her American pen friend. We corresponded for many years, and I then attended her arranged marriage to a friend of the family in Southern California, about fifteen years later.

After a few weeks I became strong enough to get back on the road to Nepal.

Following two glorious months filled with trekking in Nepal's Pokhara region, where I'd spend my 19th birthday celebrating with an international crew of fellow travelers at about 8,500 feet in the Himalaya, we flew to Paris to visit a friend. After a week we went on to stay with friends in Zurich for a couple of weeks, before returning to Montreal and then on to Boston. We arrived home on June 13, 1975, a little over eight months after we'd left home.

Upon my arrival home, Dad handed me a shoebox filled with the 76 letters I'd written to family and friends throughout those eight long months, all in chronological order.

Since then, he has periodically asked me, "Where's my book, kid?"

Well, Dad, better late than never! This is your book, dedicated to both you and Mom who said she didn't sleep through a single night during those eight months. Though I'm not in the least bit sorry I went on the trip, I do take responsibility for how difficult it must have been for you to deal with your eldest daughter traipsing across the planet with no idea if you'd ever see her again…

At one point my former husband Billy White and I were researching the possibility of honeymooning in Nepal. We visited Steve Conlon's Above the Clouds trekking company in Worcester, MA (now run by Steve's daughter out of Burlington, Vermont). When I told Steve about the copious amount of writing I'd done during that trip, he asked if his son might transcribe my letters and journals for me. Steve had spent the first half of the '70s living in Nepal and married a Nepalese woman. He wanted their half-Nepalese son to get a sense of what Nepal was like then through the eyes of a teenager. I am grateful to him for having transcribed my journal entries chronologically woven with those 76 letters to the tune of 99,000 words.

This book contains a third of the photos we took and many excerpts from that final journal I started on February 1, 1975. The journal entries are chronologically interspersed with the letters I wrote to family and friends.

As I've reviewed and read through the 99,000 words transcribed by that young man in Boston, I've been able to recognize some recurring themes.

I was devastated by the poverty in India; seeing so many dirty, starving children broke my heart. Over and over again, I'd fall in love with bright-eyed little beings and wish I could make a difference in their lives.

I'll never forget my first morning in New Delhi. It was Diwali. The holiday was celebrated with the gifting of sweets and bangle bracelets for the women, and handmade fireworks and firecrackers were fired down the crowded city streets. Dave and I stopped at a juice stand, and I had just ordered my first mango lassi. Drink in hand, I turned around to find myself confronted by five Indian women, three with two babies in their arms, and the other two holding one each. They were surrounded by at least a dozen children of assorted sizes, many tiny ones on the backs of older ones. All were dirty and wearing rags.

The hardest part was feeling the intensity of about twenty pairs of eyes imploring me to give them something.

I responded by taking the many plastic bangle bracelets I'd purchased just for this reason and handing them to the mothers. I also thrust my lassi at them and then ran down the street sobbing in overwhelm. Ridden with guilt at finding myself so privileged amongst

the squalor of some of the poorest people on the planet, I stopped to purchase a kilo of peanuts. My intention was to give them away, as I had a huge need to make whatever difference I could. But the minute I held out the bag, I was surrounded by dozens of Indian men and boys all reaching for the peanuts. Recognizing the potential danger of finding ourselves trapped by a hungry mob, Dave grabbed my hand and pulled me down the street. Instantly someone threw a cherry bomb at my feet, and the explosion was loud enough to cause my ears to ring for days. Dave took my face in his hands as one would console a crying child and said, "You can't do that here. Do you think by giving away some food you'll actually be able to change their lives? We are just hippies on a budget and can't afford to do that."

Welcome to India.

My Overland Journey

CHAPTER ONE

LEAVING HOME

GERMANY, AUSTRIA, GREECE

Wednesday, October 8 - 6:15 pm

Dear Grammy,

We arrived in Munich (Munchen as they call it) around noon on Monday. Naturally, the sky was a solid gray and it sprinkled on and off all day (and keeps raining!). Monday night we went to the famous Haufbrau haus and met some great people (Americans from NY and Texas) and two guys from New Zealand. The guys from NZ drove us to Salzburg where we are now camping across the river from the beautiful old section of town. It saved us some money (and hassles – considering neither of us speak German) getting that ride rather than taking the train.

We found out about the camp grounds being inexpensive and offering free hot showers and toilets (rather than the usual woman collecting money for use of public toilets).

After setting up our tent we walked around Salzburg. Such a lovely town but everything is so expensive! We've spent money on nothing besides food (and we look for the cheapest places), buses, and stamps. Even this postcard thing I got free at the American Express Office. We went into a bunch of incredibly beautiful churches. There sure are plenty of them, all huge, awesome, with intricately carved pews and the walls and ceiling are covered with paintings, marble statues, etc. I was completely awestruck by what I assume is Salzburg's main cathedral. Wow!

After walking around a while, we hiked up to the huge fortress overlooking the town. It's like a small walled city and we had a lot of fun exploring. The views of the city were beautiful, but the Alps are beyond belief poking through the clouds with their snow capped peaks… They looked unreal – like the backdrop in a play.

Tomorrow morning we'll head to Yugoslavia and I'll write from there. All is well here.

I Love you,
Karen

P.S. Please write to me in Nepal.

Saturday, October 12 – 8:10 pm

Dear Jeri,

Hi cutie! Here we are in rainy, cloudy, cold Yugoslavia. We've decided to take buses and trains instead of the Orient Express, so we can see more of Europe on our way across. Too bad it is the rainy season here. We just loved Salzburg but everything cost so much money! However, we did find a camping place that only cost 34 Austrian shillings per night ($2.04).

From Salzburg we went to a pretty little town called Villach. The scenery on the way there was just gorgeous! Mountains surrounded us, all with snow on them. As the road twisted and turned higher up into the Alps it grew colder and colder and there was snow everywhere! I don't speak Austrian so I didn't know how to ask the bus driver if I could jump out and make a snowball for you.

We again camped in Villach (this time it didn't cost anything because we were in a field behind a closed youth hostel). Two Swedish guys who also camped there gave us a ride to the Loiblpaf (the border) of Yugoslavia. It was really nice of them considering they weren't headed that way! They were going to a town called Klagenfurt. Anyway – here we are in Ljubljana, Yugoslavia. We're staying at a motel outside of the main town – it cost us around $7.00 and happens to be the cheapest place around. We had to take at least 5 buses to get here (you should see us getting in and out of buses with our packs always getting stuck and all the people laugh at us).

So far we've found the Yugoslavians much friendlier than either the Austrians or the Germans. All Yugoslavs must learn English in grammar school and in high school, so finding our way around is not too difficult. It's a relief finding people who speak English! My German certainly didn't get me too far – all I can say is "thank you." Every now and then my French comes in handy but not too many people speak it.

Everything in Yugoslavia is about 1/2 the price that it is in Austria. Every day for the past

5 days or so we've been buying bread, cheese, and mustard and oranges and eating only 2 meals a day – brunch and supper. Of course I treat myself to an occasional piece of torte (me and my sweet tooth) and David gets his beer. Beer is the cheapest drink around – too bad I don't really like it.

The other day, in Villach, I was walking down a side street and met four sad-looking young cows. They came up to me (other side of fence) and I sang to them and they really perked up!

Did you ever try that? Anyway – I'm having a really good time, staying healthy, and missing you and everyone else at home. Please write to me!

Love you,
Karen

Monday, October 14 - 5:00 pm

Dear everyone,

I hope Jeri got my last letter written two days ago. At the place we were staying in Ljubljana we met a really nice German guy. He and his 7-week-old German Shepherd are traveling to Istanbul in his (his name is Harold) VW bug. He asked us where we were going and to make a long story short – he wanted someone to share his travel expenses with him so we are! This way we won't be spending as much money as we would if we were taking buses and trains and we won't have to shlep our packs on and off all the time (Yeah!). So our plans have changed. At the moment we are in a rest area a little bit south of the city of "Nic" (south of Beograd). We're heading straight south to Greece (we should reach the border sometime tonight) and on through to Istanbul. I'm sure we'll have no problems being Americans in Greece – many tourists are there – and considering we're going through just in transit we're not at all worried. Anyway – I would think we'd be in Istanbul by around Oct. 20. Now we won't have to pay Bulgaria's $8 visa fee!

Harold is 24 and studying psychology. He graduates this year and plans to move to Vancouver, Canada and find a teaching job! He has friends there living in an organized commune of 2000 people. He speaks English very well and I'm really glad we found him.

So – the only problem I've had so far worth mentioning is that I lost my diary. Granted, only one week of traveling was behind me, rather than 9 months or something, but my diary was already around 30 full pages of thought! It was very neat, descriptive and had lots of pictures and food wrappers and stuff in it (done rather well if I say so myself). Oh well, I will buy myself another book somewhere in Greece.

Yugoslavia's prices are half what we paid in Germany. Thank heavens! And from Greece on everything will be even cheaper. Europe really does have icky weather. So far we've had only 1/2 a day of sunshine – and there were plenty of clouds even then. The part of Yugoslavia we've seen has been very monotonous and pretty ugly. All farm land – flat, flat, flat – an anticlimax after seeing the Alps – Aahhh. There are cows, sheep, pigs, chickens grazing everywhere we look.

We find the Yugoslavians in general much friendlier than either the Germans or the Austrians. Luckily – most everyone we've come across understands English – especially the young people as they MUST take at least four years of English in school. Mom – as I remember you mentioned that you found the Yugoslavic young people to be good looking – well they certainly are – especially the guys. The German people are pretty good looking – yet they all seem to have a cold look about them. I didn't particularly feel comfortable in either Germany or Austria. My looks stuck out like a sore thumb. Oh well – from here on I'm sure they will blend in just fine.

So far we've spent an average of $6 a day – between us – not bad considering the horrendous prices! We haven't bought ANYTHING other than food, letters and stamps – they certainly do add to some money if one writes a lot! So far I've written to all of you twice, Jeri once and Grammy once, sent a postcard to Jeffrey, and to Gail and Nancy and Linda/Jeff. I'm hoping there'll be mail waiting for me in Istanbul. I've only been away for a week now – yet so many things have happened; so many new experiences – Deutschmarks, Austrian

shillings, Yugoslavian dinars and many more to come!

You'll have to excuse my penmanship – I'm in the back of the VW along with all three backpacks and a frisky, ADORABLE puppy. These European drivers are incredible! The object of the game seems to be to pass the guy in front of you and get back in the right lane a split second before the oncoming truck in the other lane runs into you head first. Anyway – it's dark out now and writing by flashlight under these conditions is getting really tedious.

Is everyone well? Grammy? I hope so. Please write to me! I miss everyone more than I thought.

I LOVE YOU ALL!

Karen

PS My health has been absolutely great – as has my knee.

PSS. I hope all my letters are being shared with all the relatives. I do plan on writing everyone in due time.

Wednesday, October 16 (Mailed Thursday, October 17)

Mom, Dad, everyone else–

I'm so glad we came to Greece! It's such a beautiful country. The geography reminds me of Israel.

Yesterday we stopped for Turkish coffee in Thessoloniki – Greece's 2nd largest city. There I was able to purchase a new diary. However – with my other diary I lost the addresses Bob Beck so nicely compiled for me! Could you send me Bob's address so I can write him again?

After a terrifying storm last night (the wind uprooted our tent and the rain soaked everything!), today was a GORGEOUS 80 degree sunny day. I went swimming a few times – ahhh – the Aegean…

More about Greece – along the road are teeny churches – some are just big enough to look in and others fit two people. A few religious symbols like wine and oil and paintings are inside. They're so quaint!

My looks certainly do fit in here. A few people have thought I am Greek! My health is great – every day I feel myself becoming stronger.

However – I've inherited Mommy's traveling constitution (may come in handy in the east!): I go once every 3 days or so.

Some Americans we met on their way home from the East gave me a money belt to wear around my waist under my clothes. Passport and other documents in it. Bye for now!

Love,

Karen

CHAPTER TWO

THE GATEWAY TO THE EAST

ISTANBUL, TURKEY

Tuesday, October 22, 2:40 pm (7:40 am in Belmont)

Dear everyone,

We arrived in Istanbul around noon on Saturday, Oct. 19. Due to the Moslem Sabbath being Saturday and the Christian Sabbath Sunday, we didn't see Istanbul truly alive until yesterday.

On Saturday, we visited the Blue Mosque – so pretty with its mosaic and oriental rugs all over. But compared to the Topkapi Palace it was nothing! The palace is just exquisite! It's been made into a museum with an admission fee and a tourist shop. But we still enjoyed it! Displays of jewels, thrones of this sultan or that, embroidery, delft vases, porcelain, china – and all so gorgeous! We went on a tour of Sultan Murashad's harem.

He had 504 wives: four legal, 200 favorites, and 300 concubines. The Harem consists of many, many rooms – all completely done in hand painted tiles and Persian rugs – and gorgeous architecture.

We weren't as impressed with the Aya Sofia after that! You should all come to Istanbul! They have the BEST food I've ever tasted, and so cheap! Two stuffed peppers, pilaf, bread, salad, coke – only 10 liras ($.70!) And the pastry (my good old sweet tooth) baklava, everything you can think of! Delicious cheese or meat bereg – mmmmm… I'm sure not going to lose weight in this city!

We're staying in a hotel called "OTEL ANADOULO." It is situated five minutes from the Palace, 15 minutes from the Grand Bazaar, and two minutes from the famous Turkish bath. We're paying 15 Turkish liras each ($.07 to a lira) per night. Not bad considering we get hot water free! Most hotels in the area charge 20 TL per night and five lira extra for hot water!

This morning I took a Turkish bath. I walked into an ancient building. A woman asked me for 12.50 liras (about $.88), handed me a towel, soap, and shampoo, and showed me to a dressing room. For 15 liras more I could have had a massage and the works, but self service was good enough for me. I was given funny little wooden sandals to wear and directed to the sauna room. This room had a domed ceiling with all different colored glass in the different shaped holes all over it. This gives you something to look at during the fifteen minutes spent lying flat on your back upon a warm slab of marble, working up a sweat. Marble sinks with hot and cold water are all around. Then, to make sure all the soap is off, you jump into a shower in the next room. I feel so clean!!!!! Everyone should experience a Turkish bath.

Near our hotel is a place called "The Pudding Shop." It was mentioned in many of the books I looked at before my trip as being a place to meet other people traveling, to leave messages on their bulletin board, etc. It is chock-full of Westerners in dungarees traveling to or coming back from the East. Everyone there is either looking for a ride or riders to somewhere. We met a Canadian guy, Mark, who bought a 1975 VW bus in Germany. On Thursday, the three of us will head toward Nepal, sharing expenses. He will only be going as far as Herat, Afghanistan, so we will take buses from there. We anticipate a seven-day ride from here to Herat, arriving approximately next Thursday – Halloween?!

Istanbul is the most fascinating city I've ever been in! And by far the largest, except NYC. There are people everywhere, stray cats and dogs rummaging for food, horse drawn carts, buses, Mercedes, 1957 Chevy taxis, '48 Dodges, shoe shine boys and old men, men, men, men and boys everywhere! Rarely do we see women!

The grand bazaar consists of 5,000 shops all under one roof! But the prices are abominable! And compared to the Arab Market in Jerusalem, this market is a let-down. It's very Westernized; all of the stores have glass fronts, etc. In Turkey (and from here on East), one bargains for everything. People take one look at me, see me for the Westerner I am, and ask for double, triple, or even four times the real price! I'm becoming more shrewd every day. Traveling with Dave who has done this before has MANY advantages.

I sent Jeri a package from Greece. It wasn't wrapped very well because I couldn't afford the postage. As it is I paid twice as much postage than I paid for the doll! Like a dummy I stuck the two letters inside the box – they opened the box and charged me $1 or more extra because the letters weren't separate! (the bastards) I'm hoping with fingers crossed that Jeri received the package…

We had no problems in Greece. Every now and then we would tell nosy Greeks that we were Canadian to avoid possible hassles. We were traveling with Harold who is German, however, and Greeks appear to love people from Deutschland. We saw very few military personnel in Greece, but as soon as we got into Turkey (Friday afternoon), we saw army trucks and tanks everywhere! But all is quiet in Istanbul.

[This was the time of the Cyprus uprisings]

Every morning I'm awakened bright and early by a loudspeaker attached to the nearest mosque (there are mosques everywhere) blasting Salat, the ritual Moslem prayers. It sounds really eerie. They happen five times a day which takes some getting used to, as all the native people pull out their prayer rugs at the first sound of the loud speakers.

I look forward to receiving more mail from everyone when I arrive in New Delhi. Maybe you could include a little news (world and national?). The only papers we've been able to read have been British or crappy, like the Herald Tribune. All is well. I hope all is well with everyone at home. Missing you all!

Love, Karen

Wednesday, October 23 - 4:30 pm - Istanbul

Dear Grammy,

At the moment I am sitting on a low wall that surrounds a park, facing the Blue Mosque. David and I were playing Frisbee, but some guy blew a whistle and made us get off the grass (mind you, the grass is all brown and crappy anyway), so we began playing on the wide pathway. We attracted quite a number of young boys who kept saying, "Madame, Madame" and motioning for me to throw the Frisbee to them. For some reason the man with the whistle made us all leave. He was probably jealous that he couldn't play!

On my lap sits a beautiful white rabbit, and by my side are two adorable poodles, or maybe they're some kind of small terrier, I can't really tell. And also, a small Kese hound (looks like a miniature husky). All four animals belong to one young Turk. These are the first pets I have seen since I've been in Istanbul. There are thousands of stray cats and dogs all over the place. None of them looked starved, though they're all constantly searching for food. This city is very disorganized. Cars don't have any idea where they're going (their drivers that is), garbage is emptied out on street corners, so how could the animals starve? But you know me, if a kitten meows and looks up at me, I'll find something to feed it.

I know I mentioned how great the food is in my letter home, but it is worth raving about, believe me! For breakfast I have (usually) a sweet roll with a cup of tea. Everywhere, tea is served in tiny glasses and holds only about four mouthfuls. Today we were sitting in one of the 5,000 shops at the Grand Bazaar bargaining for a gorgeous Persian rug. Tea was brought to us while we sat. The man wanted $120.00

for the rug, but we weren't willing to pay more than $65. The whole city is so tourist-oriented it's sickening! A fantastic example: For lunch today, I ate stuffed peppers, tomato, onion and parsley salato, and lemonade. David had a meat dish and a beer. The normal cost should have been about 20 liras ($1.40). The waiter gave us a bill for 36 liras, thinking we're another pair of dumb, ignorant tourists. We caught him, and after arguing for 20 minutes, the bill was lowered to 24 liras. It's not the amount so much as the principle involved!

I'm glad I am traveling with a man in this part of the world. The women in these countries are suppressed, rarely let out of their homes, and the men all look at me with hungry eyes.

We've been meeting all sorts of great people. Our hotel manager is so sweet and honest! I've been told that most Turks cannot be trusted. The other night we sat in the lobby playing our flutes along with an English guy on the guitar. All the manager's friends came and clapped and had a good time. It was a nice night.

How are you feeling Grammy? Are you having to be real careful about eating? When are you due for surgery? You and everyone else are on my thoughts constantly. In the bazaar I kept seeing this rug for Shaari, that antique pin for Mom, these earrings for you, this doll for Jeri, etc. But the prices for everything were just absurd, and David repeatedly tells me things get finer and cheaper as we head east. We've been looking for something else to send Jeri as a birthday present. Tell her more (I'm hoping she received the Greek doll) will be coming soon as we travel.

Love you! Karen

Turkey to Iran

Hello everyone!

My plans change from day to day. Our ride in the 1975 VW van to Herat just didn't work out. Mark, the driver, is extremely wealthy. He inherited so much money from his grandfather that he'll never have to work. He has absolutely no conception of the value of a dollar. There were constant arguments, and I was more than glad when we left him in Tehran *(see story in the Preface on page xv)*.

Today we're taking a 22-hour bus ride to Mashhad near the Iran/Afghan border. From there we'll take another bus to Herat. Today we're going to visit the Pahlavi Museum, and I'm going to pick up some iodine or some form of water purification as the Halzone tablets take half an hour to work. By then it'll be 4:00PM and time for the bus.

I was very surprised to find Iran to be so Westernized. Everyone dresses very Western, but ironically enough, the women all wear long shawls hiding everything except their eyes. Oct. 26 was the Shah's birthday and everywhere I look I see Christmas lights. The Iranians really worship their Shah. On all buses, trucks, coins, bills, store fronts, EVERYWHERE, there are pictures of him. On TV there's either a soccer game or the Shah (although last night we saw Ironsides dubbed in Persian)!

In Turkey we paid $10.50 to fill the gas tank in the van. In Iran it only cost us $4.50! However, the cost of living is a bit higher in Iran than in Turkey. Everything here seems more organized and is definitely much cleaner. The bathrooms are Eastern style of course, but they're usually kept pretty clean and sometimes there's even a bar of soap!

It's hard to believe we're still on the same planet in some ways. The terrain driving from Turkey to Iran is incredible! There are mountains everywhere, all brown and weirdly shaped.

There are herds of cows, sheep, goats, donkeys, horses everywhere! As we approached the Iranian border, 19,000 ft. high Mt. Ararat was visible with its snow-covered peak. It's a good 9,000 feet higher than any of the surrounding mountains and the only one with snow on it. It's quite a sight to behold!

We had expected the weather to be cold this time of year, but today in Tehran it's about 70 degrees, as it has been since we entered Greece! We haven't seen a bit of rain since Yugoslavia! Afghanistan should be a bit colder, especially at night. Pakistan and northern India should be pretty warm, and Nepal should be warm during the days, and maybe the temp will drop below freezing at night depending on altitude.

All during our trip we've been coming across fellow travelers. Australians, Germans, English, New Zealanders, Swiss, Italian, Canadian, and everyone is either going toward or coming from the East. It certainly does seem to be the thing to do. I haven't met a person yet who doesn't agree that Nepal is the best country in the world. The Nepalese people are reputed to be extremely happy, always singing as they work, etc. And they're an honest people, unlike their neighbors in India, Pakistan, etc., where nothing is safe unless under lock and key!

As the days go by I'm seeing and experiencing so many new things and learning so much about people and about myself. Everywhere we've gone so far, we've found people who speak English. It's taught in schools (and is a mandatory course) in Yugoslavia, Iran, Greece… Here in Iran, everyone speaks English! Believe me, this does make life a bit simpler.

I haven't much else to say for the time being – all is well with us. I've had a minor case of diarrhea but nothing serious. The food in Turkey was so good that I managed to GAIN a little weight. Oh well, I'm sure I'll lose it soon enough. Please write to me in Kathmandu!

Love, Karen

CHAPTER THREE

HALLOWEEN IN HERAT

AFGHANISTAN

Herat, Afghanistan (Halloween)
Monday, October 31

Hello everyone!

Coming into Afghanistan was like stepping back 200 years in time. This place is amazing, so timeless. Herat has a population of 100,000, and it is Afghanistan's second largest city! Everything is dusty; all the land around is barren and mountainous and the winds blow off the topsoil, spreading it over everything. The city just grows out of the earth. All resources are utilized. Their telephone poles are trees that just happen to be growing there. There are no imported goods used for building – the people utilize every bit of wood (which isn't much) and have to use cow dung mixed with hay as fuel for their fires.

The weather here is gorgeous! Never a cloud in the sky, and the temp is around 80, with a nice breeze and the extremely hot Afghan sun beating down. At night it drops down to around 45 degrees, which is really refreshing. We're staying at about the cleanest place in town, called the "Mahmon" Hotel, but known to Westerners as the "Lemone Squash Hotel" (Lemone Squash is a very popular English drink). The menu here is more extensive than any menu in the city!

Here's a sample from a local restaurant's menu:

*Afs: abbreviation for Afghanis – the currency here – One Afghani = 1.8 cents

2 Fried Eggs	12 Afs*
Omelet	12 Afs
Yogurt	5 Afs
Nan	2 Afs
Chips (French fries)	10 Afs
Coke, orange	10 Afs
Chai (of course)	3 Afs
Coffee	4 Afs
" w/ milk	5 Afs
Rice, potato, and spinach (ugh)	15 Afs

I've been eating a lot of eggs and nan – which is a loaf of oval shaped bread, about 1/2 inch thick, a foot long, and 6" wide – made of wheat, which I buy fresh outside of the stove it's made in and costs only 2 Afs. There's a lot of fruit being sold: grapes, pears, melons, pomegranates. We've had the best melons! Cantaloupes shaped like footballs, with green and yellow striped skin, and sweet. And Debbie, I'm now drinking more tea than you could possibly consume! A pot of tea is served for 3 Afs, and there is enough to fill the little tea glass they give you four times. But because the climate is extraordinarily dry, I'm retaining all my fluids. After 8 cups of tea and a coke, I still don't have to go! At our hotel there's hot water, which is pretty rare, but it feels so good!

It's difficult to write because there's so much to say. Everything here is different from anything I've ever seen or imagined. Herat may be the second largest city, but rarely does a car drive by. Sometimes a beautifully painted lorry (open-backed trucks) passes at breakneck speed, but usually all one sees are donkeys carrying heavy loads of hay, wood, or maybe 1 or 2 people and horse-drawn rickshaws, which resemble Roman chariots.

Men with turbans are everywhere. They all wear long baggy shirts down to their knees, called a Peram, with baggy pajama-like trousers of the same color. A sport jacket or blanket, sweater, scarf, etc. are also worn. Many men are barefoot. Others wear old plastic shoes with an occasional leather pair here and there. Never does one see a woman! Any women in the street are TOTALLY covered by a chaderi (aka burkha). They look like walking pyramids with the black cloth covering their entire body, including their heads and faces, with only a screen for them to look through. They stare at me, as does everyone here, and scurry away when I say hello. An occasional old man has spit at my feet (I'm told it's because I'm a grown woman and my head isn't covered).

And the children are everywhere, dressed in their dirty clothing. Their big brown innocent eyes just stare at me and they say "Allo meester baksheesh?" and a dirty little hand is held out. Baksheesh means "gift" – money usually.

Instead of giving out money I like to give food. Sometimes I'll give out peanuts; just carrying the bag around draws people!

November 2

HAPPY BIRTHDAY JERI! I do hope you got the Greek doll I sent you! I've been thinking about you a lot, remembering when I was nine and stood up in Miss Stathos' 4th grade during show and tell and said, "I have a new baby sister!" Wow, that was so long ago, and yet it seems so recent! You've really grown up! It's really difficult to write letters while I'm in transit. I don't want you to worry when you don't hear from me for awhile – though from now on I'll try to warn you. This letter probably won't be mailed until I get to Kabul in a few days.

I hear the local people steam off the stamps to use them again, and many letters just don't make it out of the country. When I bought this paper, they were out of aerogrammes. Anyway, my aerogramme will be a lot more informative.

Love, Karen

Friday, November 8

Dear Jeri,

Disregard the brown paper note – I was in a big hurry when I wrote it. In the package is a white embroidered shirt which is handmade and I hope it fits you. Also, the mirrored cap is for you, not necessarily to wear. All the Afghani men and boys wear gaily decorated caps – some embroidered, some with beads, some like the one in your package. I was looking everywhere for one, and as I was walking from one shop to another, a man came up and showed me this cap. It is very old; it probably was in the man's family for many years, but he needed money. If you'd like one of the little

purses, help yourself. They are very old, made by Kuchis, the nomads of Afghanistan. Tell Laurie and David they may each choose one. Please keep the other stuff in a safe place until I get home. I have to send this by land and sea instead of airmail because it is so expensive by air. I hope this reaches you soon!

Write to me honey!

Love,

Karen

Kabul, Afghanistan
Friday, November 8

Dear Mom and Dad,

I have so many things to say that it's difficult to write. We arrived in Kabul on Tuesday night, November 5. Such a fascinating city! It has a population of 3 million (there are a total of 16 million people in Afghanistan). There's a total mixture of new and old here.

We're staying in what is called the Sharenau section of town, where there are plenty of good restaurants and hotels, and everything is so inexpensive relative to our travel budget. We've eaten at the Mercedes Restaurant. I ordered a vegetable dinner, and I got a bowl of delicious homemade veggie soup, bread, French fries, roast potato, rice, boiled carrots, beets, tomato, and lettuce. Everything was either peeled or boiled and so good! And a banana milkshake… mmm… and the whole thing cost $.70! The handicrafts are amazing, and I'm wanting to buy everything I see. So far I've only bought a skirt for myself (the one I had made) and a few very old embroidered pouches made by the Kuchis (Afghanistan's nomads).

I'm glad I read James Michener's *Caravans* as it gives one a pretty good picture of this amazing country. Actually, no sort of introduction could have totally prepared me for so many new things at once. Suddenly, no one speaks English except for some shop keepers in tourist districts. Their English is limited to prices and "For you meestah, veddy, veddy cheap!" is heard constantly. I've definitely got the knack for bargaining as from Istanbul on East everything from food to hotel rooms is bargained for. We also bought four hand-embroidered shirts, which I am mailing home tomorrow along with the purses and a beautifully embroidered shirt for Jeri. It was very hard to judge the size as she grows so fast. I'll have to mail them by sea because for a package weighing one kilo it costs 800 Afs ($16) by air mail! I haven't decided whether or not I'll keep the shirts; I'll probably sell a couple for a good profit. Also in the package is a very old Afghani cap. All the men and boys wear decorated caps to shield their heads from the strong sun.

We spent a good part of yesterday at the American center in the library. The most recent paper was the *Christian Science Monitor* from probably be entering India at the Amritsar crossing on Tuesday. From Amritsar we'll catch a train to Delhi – another 12 hours!! So we should be in Delhi by Friday. And I'm looking forward to there being mail for me from home!

A month may not seem very long to you, but so much has happened during my month of traveling! Germany, Austria, Yugoslavia,

Oct. 28. What happened with the elections??? I'm sorry I couldn't vote. All I've heard is that John Glenn is now a senator in Ohio. Please write me all that is happening. I hear Nixon was on the critical list? And is inflation worse every day? I do wish I'd told you to write me in Kabul. We're leaving here Sunday morning at 7:30. We'll be in Peshawar, Pakistan at around 3:00 PM that day and will catch a bus immediately to Lahore, another 12 hours or so. We'll

Greece, Turkey, Iran, Afghanistan – WOW! I've been thinking about home and how much I really do love all of you. Now I look back and think, Why did I give up piano, flute, studying, oh – so many things? And treat you two (the people who love me and know me more than anyone in this world…) like dirt? I owe you such an apology for so many things. Somehow the reality of Afghanistan, including the people and their simple way of living, has brought me down to earth.

I'm eighteen years old, and I've left home, though home is a place I think I'll be spending some time at in the near future. I should get to

know my family better than I ever have. I know that I always ran here, there, not really caring where, as long as it was away from having to think about myself. But now I'm thinking and thinking and learning more about me every day.

There are just so many things I have to say to you. I miss you both and Debbie and Jeri and Kitty. How is Grammy? At times being this far away is a little scary, no denying that. I've been doing a lot of writing in my diary and I write home as often as possible; it's very difficult while we're in transit.

All is going great with Dave and me. We're constantly meeting people from all over the world! Yesterday, while I was reading the paper, a 19-year-old Afghani girl, Zabila, asked if I had time to help her with her English lesson. She was trying to write a story and needed lots of help. Today Zabila, Dave, and I climbed the 800 foot hill in the center of Kabul. I helped her write a letter in English to her boyfriend, telling him she would marry him. I guess he had asked her a number of times but she'd said "No" not feeling ready. She's the first Afghani

woman (over the age of 8) that I've spent any time with. So many women still wear chaderies (burkhas), which I find so sad! When I say

hello (salaam) to them, most scurry away. Yet I can feel them staring at me from behind their screens…

Surprisingly enough (considering all the rumors I've heard), I haven't been at all sick.

I've been very careful. I haven't had even one sip of any unpurified water. I'm eating a pretty balanced diet, though I'm staying away from meat as much as possible. Nuts are very cheap and are a good source of protein. I hear that this time of year is the best for fruits and veggies in Pakistan and India. I've been eating pomegranates, cantaloupes, watermelons, and mandarin oranges all along the way.

Dave and I are getting along wonderfully, and when we feel like talking to others and being with others, there are always other Westerners around. We've met up with a couple from Ohio who spent time with Dave on his last trip. They're really neat people, as are so many of the other people around. For a little while we were with Lloyd, on sabbatical from his job as a philosophy teacher at a small college in Toronto. He's 59 years old and traveling the

same route we are! His wife is home in Toronto. I'm running out of room on this aerogramme. I want you to know I am well, loving you, missing you, and thinking and learning more and more every day.

Saturday, November 9 - Morning

Dear Grammy,

So much is happening all the time! So many new experiences. At the moment I am sitting in "Alice's Restaurant" in Afghanistan's bustling capital, Kabul. All the restaurants and hotels in this area are extremely cheap, catering to hippie travelers like us. We stopped at a bakery (the sweets here are great – they must have seen me coming!) and picked up an apple turnover, a doughnut, and a few assorted others.

The other day we went to the Kabul museum. It is full of very old Buddhist artifacts, carved ivory, and a lot of interesting information about the history of Afghanistan. This place is ageless! The whole country I mean. There are still thousands of nomads, called Kuchis, roaming the country, following the seasons. Over the ages they have made incredibly beautiful handicrafts, many of which are on sale in the shops all around. I wish I could afford to buy everything and anything I see, especially some of the jewelry. And yesterday I saw a gorgeous handmade soap-stone chessboard. Daddy would've loved it, but I've heard there are beautiful ivory chess boards all over New Delhi for about the same price, so I'll wait. We'll be in Delhi in a few days. The days sure are flying by, and we want to reach Nepal while it's still somewhat warm! Though I don't expect we should (or could possibly) be there before the 3rd week in November, which brings me to thoughts about Thanksgiving. This will be the first time I won't be home for it, which does make me pretty sad.

How are you, Grammy? I hope you're not in any discomfort! I think of home and everyone so often that at times I'm a bit torn. But this journey I'm taking is amazing. I'm meeting so MANY different kinds of people. There's a tremendous number of Westerners on the road from countries like Germany, Austria, Holland, Scandinavia, Canada, France, Italy! And I now know at least one person from every state, I think. We're never the only Westerners on a bus, and our hotels are filled with young travelers like ourselves.

The children around are really beautiful. They're dressed in all sorts of ways. Some wear the traditional (comfortable) Afghani baggy shirts and pants and gaily decorated cap. Others are dressed in more Western clothing. You wouldn't believe the clothing bazaars! There are piles and piles of cast-off Western apparel – every style, size, and shape you've ever seen in your life – for so cheap!

I bought a pair of good thick nylon socks which come way above my knee – I only paid $.20 for them! Absolutely anything goes here. I've seen children walking around in a pair of pajamas! As we get to the outskirts of town, more and more beggars appear. Some of them are REALLY poor, and it hurts my heart not to be able to help them.

Yesterday David, Zabila (an Afghani girl I met), and I climbed the 800 ft. hill in the center of Kabul. Halfway up the mountain was a little boy flying a kite he'd made himself out of a plastic bag and some sticks. The look on his face was of sheer joy. He ran up and down the hillside (and believe me, it is VERY steep with loose rocks; he moved like a little mountain goat!). As he paused to take in some of the slack, I gave him some peanuts and Dave let him look though the binoculars. I don't think that child will forget yesterday for a long time, and neither will I!

Every day my love for children grows stronger and stronger. Many children ask me for pens or pencils, which I don't have to give. Before we go trekking in Nepal, I'm going to pick up a bunch of pencils to give to the children we'll meet along the way. Also, we have 3 Frisbees to give away. Knowing how practical the people here are, the Frisbee would probably be used as a plate!

I hope all my mail has reached home – I do wish I were able to write more often. Post offices are open weird hours, and sometimes we're not in a place long enough to even get to a post office! Banks are a real pain in the neck – so much red tape to go through! It takes at least 45 minutes to change one traveler's cheque! We have been spending quite a bit of money – about $250 each – NOT including the Persian rugs we sent home. From here on we won't be spending that much because the East is still really cheap. Can you imagine paying less than $.50 a night for a decent hotel with hot water, clean (Eastern style of course) toilets, and a lovely garden? Well we are! I'm having a lot of fun and learning an amazing amount all the time, much of it about myself. I hope all is well and can't wait to find a letter from you when we reach Delhi, Benares, and/or Nepal! Love you and miss you!

Karen

Pakistan - Briefly!

We arrived in Peshawar, Pakistan at around 5:30 (setting our watches ahead another 1/2 hour to local time). At 7:00 PM (still Sunday), we boarded another bus to Lahore, arriving at 5:45 AM. We had been traveling with Kay, a 35-year-old ex-school teacher from California. She decided to spend some time in Lahore, but we took another bus to the Pakistan-Indian border. The whole time I wasn't feeling too well, having had a mild case of dysentery. I was sick from Saturday night until Tuesday morning. Yuck! At the Pakistan-Indian border I had to lie down in the Indian customs office! A Swiss guy gave me some dysentery pills called "Carbantren," and they worked really well. The paregoric didn't seem to help at all (and boy does it taste yucky!).

From Amritsar, India we took a night train to Delhi, arriving at 7:00 AM Tuesday morning. Only yesterday? It feels like we've been here for weeks! It was great receiving mail! I got two letters from you, Mom, one from you, Jeri, and one from Grammy. Unfortunately, we didn't visit Abdul, Dave's friend in Pakistan. We spent only a matter of hours there (in the country), aboard buses the whole time. I hope you'll write, Deb. By the way, Jeri mentioned your hand getting cut – I hope it's all right! And Dad, please write to me.

On Friday we're going to Agra to see the Taj Mahal. We're taking the Taj Express especially for tourists as that's the only way to get there from Delhi. Too bad I don't like Indian food, because Western food runs into a bit of

money (again, cheap compared to home…). A typical Indian meal consists of white rice, flat wheat-flour bread called chapati, and of course a curry dish. Mom, your curries are as different from Indian curries as black is from white! Here, they are so spicy I can't handle more than one mouthful! Like nothing I've ever tasted. I HAD to drink half a glass of water (the first unpurified water I've had since Greece!). But this is the season (if there is one) to be in India. The fruits amaze me: mangoes, bananas, tangerines, apples, melons, grapes, nuts. And it's all so cheap! 5 tangerines for 1 rupee. A really healthy delicious drink served everywhere is Lassi. It's yogurt mixed with water (blended) and sugar or salt or plain, depending on individual tastes. It's the best thirst-quenching drink I've ever had.

This time of year the weather is really fine. During the day it gets pretty hot, but I'm comfortable in my long skirt and loose Afghani embroidered shirt. I wear my hair in braids, as it stays out of the way and keeps me cooler. I'm so glad I brought my earth shoes. We do lots of walking in the city – about 5 or 6 miles today – and I never get tired (We do walk in the shade whenever possible.)! David wears a pair of pants and a baggy Afghan shirt, called a Peram, with a use-for-everything scarf around his neck. As his beard comes in better and he gets tanned, he looks more and more Eastern. We're both really healthy. I only wash my hair about once every five or six days. Mommy, you wouldn't believe how healthy it's gotten! Thicker, shinier, and it stays clean much longer! Every day we're taking vitamins A, B, C, and E, and I'm feeling really fine.

CHAPTER FOUR

WELCOME TO INDIA

DELHI AND BENARES (VARANASI)

Wednesday, November 13 – 9:15 pm

And now we find ourselves in Delhi where Diwali is being celebrated. It's the Hindu equivalent to Christmas in terms of being the biggest Hindu holiday of the year. Sitting in my hotel room, it sounds as though the city is being bombed! Firecrackers are sold everywhere, and some of them are like small bombs. The people are going crazy! Our hotel is situated smack in the middle of the grand bazaar in New Delhi. The room is pretty nice and is costing us 16 rupees a night (8 rupees to 1 dollar). India is nowhere near as cheap as Afghanistan.

When I walk out of the hotel I am confronted by so much activity! People everywhere, shops of all sorts where everything imaginable is sold. Can you imagine being in the middle of a fairly modern city with cars, stop lights, thousands of people, and seeing loads of BIG white Brahma cows (with scary-looking horns) roaming around, eating anything they please, going anywhere they wish? Traffic stops for them, people walk by and touch them on the head; you see, cows are holy (Who knows why? I just know that cows are considered – by Hindus – to be a reincarnate of the God Krishna). They just meander about, seemingly totally apathetic to all that is happening around them. And believe me, much is happening! There are all sorts of taxis around. Horse-drawn rickshaws, little three-wheeled cars that putt around the city, old World War II Harley-Davidson motorcycles (they're really big), probably from the States or England, which have been converted into taxis by the addition of a car's rear axle and drive shaft and a four- or five-passenger carriage on top. And of course they're gaily decorated, as are all the others.

And the people… it really is amazing how many there are. 650 million in the country, and India is only 1/3 the size of the US! I've seen

a lot of beggars, some of whom are in pretty bad shape. It is very difficult for me and puts a slight damper on everything I do. I've been giving away money; to each person I try to give 10 or 25 paisa (there are 100 paisa in a Rupee), but today I bought a bunch of plastic bangle bracelets that all the women and girls wear and gave them out to little girls who didn't seem to be having a very happy Diwali.

I also gave out a 1/2 kilo of peanuts. I much prefer giving food than money. There aren't any starving people around although many look pretty hungry. Many lepers are on the streets; some have no fingers and toes; others have messed up facial features. Sometimes they have fresh bandages with iodine stains upon them, but usually their bandages are as dirty as they are. I feel so lucky for my health and resources. From Turkey on East I've noticed many people with one bad eye. This is due to the fact that the eye is a really vulnerable part of the body, and these countries are very dusty. So here in India just about all the people – babies, old men, etc. – wear eye liner as it's sticky and collects the dust particles. David and I also are wearing it.

Nov. 14 - 10:40am

Good morning! Despite the firecrackers and bombs and people shouting that went on all night, I had a great sleep. Walking all day makes me so tired. Everything is so cheap that we're able to live like kings: going out to restaurants for 3 meals a day, having our clothes washed by someone (I'm not that lazy, we only had someone wash our dungarees because they hadn't been washed for so long and I had access only to cold water). However, we have been spending too much money; all the little things begin to add up! I want to send everyone things I see, but the postage is just too expensive. I sent Jeri a package from Afghanistan; I regret having sent it from there, because it's more expensive than from India, and it probably won't ever reach Jeri. Someone will most likely open it up, like what he sees, and decide to keep it. Those are the breaks.

I just finished reading *A Different Woman* by Jane Howard, an autobiography. Such a beautiful book. You should all read it! Here's my breakfast: two fried eggs and toast and tea. I have to eat a lot of eggs for protein, as I like to stay away from meat. In India, it's a lot easier to do so because Hindus are vegetarians. They eat dal lentils for protein. They eat so many carbs! Rice, potatoes, bread, and cauliflower with curry is typical.

As I've said before, I'm keeping a good diary; it's more of a scrapbook, actually. All sorts of labels, train tickets, etc. are pasted in. I'm loving to write, and I find myself composing sentences and thoughts in my head constantly, even when I'm walking through a bazaar. The number of people here is pretty incredible. I literally have to push my way down a street – sometimes pedestrian traffic comes to a dead halt! Here in India they drive on the left side of the road (because of the British being here for so long). Many of the people speak English, and there are more signs in English than Hindi.

Today we have a lot to do. I'm getting my smallpox vaccination, and we have to reserve seats for tomorrow's train to Agra and for Sunday's train to Benares, where we will spend the night (maybe 2 nights) before heading to Kathmandu. We should be in Kath.

by Wednesday. Today we want to go to the American library to catch up on some news. I'm hoping there will be a Boston paper so I can find out who's governor, etc. It's difficult to get American papers while traveling – ooh! A little mouse just ran by, stopped, took one look at me, and took off under the bed. There's also a teeny lizard living in our wall. No bugs though! There's so much to say, but no more space – write to Kathmandu quickly!

Benares (now called Varanasi)
Sunday, November 17

Dear Grammy,

And now I am in Benares, the holiest city in India. We took a 17-hour night train from New Delhi. What a hellish ride! 3rd class has been abolished by the Indian government, so there are only two classes – 1st and 2nd. We ride 3rd (it's called 2nd class, but it's so lousy I have to say 3rd) as it's so cheap. Only wooden benches, but we have our foam rubber pads to use. Anyway, I'm really glad to be out of Delhi – such a big, noisy, smoggy city! And it's very Westernized.

Yesterday we went to the Parliament to apply for visas into the country of Sikkim, which is an Indian protectorate. The Himalayas run right through Sikkim, and since very few Westerners have been there, it should be fascinating!

Here in Benares everything is so Eastern. No signs in English (whereas there were many more signs in and people speaking English than Hindi in Delhi due to the British control for so many years. You should hear the Hindi-British accent – what a riot!). Ninety percent of the traffic is made up of humans, and the rest

are bicycle rickshaws (there are only a few cars and buses). Riding from the train station to our hotel (about 4 miles) cost us only four rupees, and the poor guy had to pedal the two of us and our packs! (400 lb. about!)

So many things are happening here… the Ganges River (holiest river in the world) runs through the city, and by its side are burning ghats for the dead. Religious Hindus walk hundreds of miles to die in Benares so that their

ashes may be thrown in the Holy River. There certainly are a lot of really old people around… And all over India are beggars. Every time the train stopped, beggars would come to the windows with their dirty hands outstretched, and others walk through the train, exposing sores and some are blind, etc. I give what I can, though it gets a little ridiculous. I wish I could do more for the people. 10,000 people LIVE at Calcutta's train station.

What upsets me the most is how many rich Indians there are… Women in gorgeous silk saris, Sikhs with their Western clothes looking so above it all! They have so much yet seem to give nothing to others. The caste system may have been legally abolished, but in real life it's still very much apparent. Many Westerners are able to harden themselves toward the poverty, but not me. Every hungry person I see upsets me more than the last.

Before I forget – I had a smallpox vaccination at a hospital in Delhi; I'm having a nice healthy reaction to it. Also, in Delhi I picked up a really nice beautiful sandalwood chess set for Mom and Dad's anniversary. In order to mail the chess set, I had to wait in line for ½ an hour in a hot, stuffy post office filled with Indians (by the way, the majority of Indians I've met tend to be on the stupid side), only to get to the front of the line and find out I needed to fill out four forms (I could've had that done while I waited in line!). And then to the back of the line again for another 45 minutes. By this time my patience was running a bit thin… Finally, after having my package weighed and

having to wait in another line to buy stamps and back to the first line to have it stamped and to get my receipt – I COULDN'T mail it without my passport! My passport was at the Nepalese Embassy for my visa to Nepal. I lost my temper and yelled at the guy… What more did he want? Of course, he only laughed… Anyway, I hope the package gets there soon! Before this letter!

And now I am sitting on the little balcony outside our hotel room overlooking a side street about a 15-minute walk from the center of town. Considering the tremendous numbers of people who live in Benares, this street is really quiet. It's about 9:15 PM, and people are settling down. The little chai shop across the street is still open for business. Tea (chai) is served everywhere. It's always made with milk and sugar and tastes so good and only costs 30 paisa (about 3 cents!)! This room, which is clean and good-sized and even has a table and 2 chairs, is only costing us 5 rupees each per night. There are about 9 rupees to one US dollar. The dollar is still the most favored currency in the east. In Delhi we changed some of the cash we brought on the black market. We got 9 rupees per $ and the bank rate is only 8 Rs. per $1. Everywhere we go, guys ask us if we have cash to change.

Back to me. Tonight I had a refreshing cold shower (hot showers are seldom available), and we had a delicious meal at a Chinese restaurant. The food was very different than the American-style Chinese food, but equally as good.

I'm writing more and more – and enjoying doing so more than ever! My diary is already almost half full! I write home as often as possible while I'm in transit. I'm anxious to get mail – to hear how you are – how the operation went – how is everyone? How was Jeri's party? How is Jeri, and Deb? I hope she'll write… I hope you all have written, and a bunch of mail awaits me in Kathmandu. I had hoped to get some today here in Benares. It was a bit of a let down… I'll check again tomorrow. I'm missing everyone so very much – loving everyone and appreciating them – and thinking of you and wishing to see you – but I'm learning so much where I am – so much about myself and the world. There's a man in the street below who's ironing 2 pairs of pants. His iron: he has a metal oven (shoe-box sized) with burning coals inside and a cover with a handle. Everything is so old-fashioned, so down to earth – so nostalgic of days gone by. Grammy, I love your letters – you always have written such nice stories. Please write!

Love,
Karen

CHAPTER FIVE

THANKSGIVING IN KATHMANDU

KATHMANDU

Thanksgiving 1974 - 11:15 pm

Dear Mom, Dad, Jeri, Debbie,

I'm feeling very full after a Thanksgiving feast of sweet and sour chicken, vegetable fried rice, and tea, followed by a piece of coconut cream pie. Kathy and Jeff, who are an American couple from Ohio, whom David and Cedric met two years ago at the base of Mt. Everest, and have also returned to Nepal. Anyway, the four of us are really good friends, and we're going trekking together. We've decided to trek from Bodhnath (5 km. from Kathmandu) to Gosainkund Lake (about 4 days hike) which is 14,373 ft. We'll take it real slow; we (me especially) aren't in very good physical condition. Riding buses and trains for 6 weeks tends to drain one a bit. From Gosainkund, we will trek the 5 or so days to Langtang Valley. And then, providing snow hasn't made the going too difficult, we plan to go over Ganga La, which is a 16,803 ft. pass for which we will need a guide. I openly admit that I'm a little scared, but I know that trekking is the best thing I could be doing.

It's like an Outward Bound course, only much more realistic. We've been buying food to carry with us for the 6 or so days when we

won't be passing through any villages. Rice, bournita, powdered milk, garlic, onions, peanut butter, crackers, cheese, and for vitamin C the only thing available is raisins (oranges wouldn't keep in our packs), and they cost 4 rupees for 100 grams! (There are eleven Nepalese rupees to the dollar.) In case any of us begin to get any sort of altitude sickness, we'll immediately turn back – though I am bringing some pills called Lasix, and of course I'll be taking vitamins A, B, C, and E for two out of our 3-week journey. We'll be walking through little settlements and villages, where food will be available. We'll be getting up around 6:00, drinking tea (or bournita), trekking until 10:00, when we will have a big meal. And then at about noon we'll start walking. At about 4:00, toward the end of a day we will stop in a village to eat and sleep. For $.30 one gets rice, potatoes, maybe sabji (vegetables) with curry on everything and of course, chai. Here chai is usually served with milk and sugar boiled into it. After the meal, you can stay there for nothing, so the tents won't be used every night. And I'll be able to get to know the people! Nepali is only slightly similar to Hindi, but I have learned a few basic phrases. I'm very glad I took those Hindi lessons; they've helped me out quite a bit! The Nepalese people are beautiful! The women all have braids below their waists and wear a special dress which sort of wraps all around and covers their whole bodies – usually they're black and a gaily colored woven belt is worn around the waist.

Yesterday, David, Kathy, Jeff, and I rented bikes and rode to Patan, which is a Tibetan refugee camp 5 kilometers from Kathmandu. As we rode out of the city, things grew really rural, nothing Western or familiar, no machinery of any kind. Only people; people with beautiful oriental faces, browned by years of mountain sunshine, always smiling! The refugee camp is situated a little above Kathmandu (4290 ft), and there's a better view of the mountains. All around Kathmandu Valley are 5,000

HITCHHIKING TO KATHMANDU: MY OVERLAND ODYSSEY, 1974

ft. mountains, with 7 or 8 thousand-footers behind them, and off in the distance, enshrouded by clouds and shooting above everything are the white snow-capped peaks of the Himalaya – the WORLD'S highest mountains. The views we're going to have while we're trekking… I'm really getting excited. We're leaving Saturday and should be back around the 20th of December. We'll stay here for a few days and then head to Pokhara, the only other city in Nepal. I've heard many good things about Pokhara – 25,000 ft. mountains are only 15 miles away from the city! Did I mention that Roy Norsigian is also in Kathmandu?

It was quite something to see someone from home here, even though we knew we'd see Roy. I think of everyone at home and wonder how each of you would react to traveling in the East.

Back to the Tibetan Refugee camp; we visited a Tibetan rug factory where about 100 people of all ages and sexes were weaving incredible carpets, all of them singing softly in a high-pitched nasal voice. So strange… so far away from anything I've ever dreamed of… and a little man with a wispy goatee and a toothless smile held up 2 hand-sized Lhasa Apso puppies – they're precious! And in the states they cost $300! Speaking of prices, are they still steadily increasing? Tomorrow I'm going to the American Center to read a few papers.

We have visa extensions until Jan. 4, and possibly (probably) we'll be in Nepal longer than that. It's a fascinating place. One easily loses all sense of time here, as I experience and learn so much all the time. After Pokhara for a few days, we're going to trek to the Annapurna sanctuary, a grass field (12,500 ft.) surrounded by 26,700 ft. mountains! That will only be a 7 day trek all together. From Pokhara we'll return to Kathmandu and then perhaps on to Darjeeling, though we'd like to be in

Kathmandu for the King's coronation in late February. However, we've heard that no tourists (especially young ones like us) are wanted here during that time. All over the city, buildings are being repaired and painted, and in a big field, people are rehearsing for the coronation ceremony. So… write again to the Am. Exp. Office here in Kathmandu. Now you won't be hearing from me for 3 weeks but don't worry, I'll be in the mountains and I'm very well equipped for my journey. I love you all. Happy Chanukah. I felt a bit lonely tonight; hope Thanksgiving was nice…

Love, Karen

HAPPY ANNIVERSARY – I hope you received my gift – HAPPY NEW YEAR!

Kathmandu
Friday, November 22

Dear Debbie,

I'm in Kathmandu, sitting in David's and my hotel room sharing travel stories with Roy! We stayed in Benares for 2 1/2 days after a terrible train ride from Delhi. At one point, I had some sesame candy in my lap, and something came up and grabbed a piece! At first I thought it was some really daring kid, but I turned and saw a big, ugly, light brown monkey! Suddenly I was surrounded by monkeys – little ones, some

bigger than the four-year-old boy whose apple he grabbed, scaring the poor kid half to death. And Hare Krishna people chanted behind me, all sorts of people walking by with various paint on their faces. Dead people covered with cloth were carried by; the burning of the dead is the most sacred ritual in Hinduism. Men are wrapped in white, women in bright colors; all that remains of the bodies are the ashes, men's chest bones, and women's hip bones, all of which are scattered in the Ganges – boy is it polluted.

There is this place called the "Upper Crust Pie Shop" over on Pig Street. There are pie shops everywhere and big hairy pigs roaming around and cows and children and dogs… Such a heavy place! Anyway – lemon meringue, German chocolate cake, pineapple upside down cake, chocolate cream pie, coconut chiffon, brownies, coffee cake, apple pie, mixed fruit pie, cherry pie, apricot pie, you name it! All the pies are scrumptious – as good as anything you or Grammy or anyone else has made – though I do hope you took a picture of that cake you made for Jeri. Her party sounded great! I hope by now Mom and Dad have received the chess set, and I hope they can find a board for it. I couldn't find one. I wish I could send everyone some of the beautiful things I've seen, but postage is too expensive and such a pain in the neck to go through.

I'm thinking about a lot of people. I was so relieved and happy to get mail today. I got some in Istanbul and Delhi – but missed it in Benares. I got both your letters – they're beautiful – they tell me so much about you. I feel closer to you somehow, as I do to everyone now that I feel I've been accepted by you all for what I am. I'm learning so much about me and everything, so much about life. The Nepalese people always smile and they're so beautiful… And the mountains…

Love, Karen

Sunday, November 24 - Morning

Dear Grammy,

This city is really amazing – about 1/2 of it is freaks – young people from all over the world – everyone into different things – hiking, religion, vegetating, photography, drugs, studying, writing – you name it and we've met someone doing it. Also, I've met people from just about all the states, including Alaska and Hawaii. The majority of travelers seem to come from the US, Germany, England, France, Japan – countries with relatively high economies, where it isn't difficult to earn and save money. The other half of the people here in Kathmandu are Nepalese. All of the Nepalese people are nice – smiling, mellow. Such a contrast from India, where all of the people are really uptight. I didn't like India at all – the only thing I'll go back to see is the Taj Mahal, which we had to miss this time because the train was filled up.

Let me tell you about the great day I had yesterday: Our friend Roy Norsigian from Watertown (he and Dave have been friends for 8 yrs) left the states in June, spending 5 months or so in Pakistan and Afghanistan. And now he also is in Nepal and we're all together (along with a great couple from Ohio who David and

I have spent a lot of time with since we met them in Istanbul). David and they (Kathy and Jeff) had met up 2 years ago at the base of Mt. Everest! Anyway, after a delicious breakfast of fruit salad (oranges, bananas, and papayas), two fried eggs, toast, and coffee, Roy, David and I headed toward Swayambhu, where the monkey temple is on the outskirts of the city. A 25 minute walk through narrow streets filled with Nepalese (you wouldn't believe how beautiful the children are!), cows, water buffaloes, goats, dogs, pigs… Such beautiful weather – 75 degrees during the day – sun shining and the sky is amazingly blue – at night it drops to about 40, but I have my warm parka to put on. We climbed the hill leading to Swayambhu (pretty steep but not difficult or long – there's a long staircase). We stopped halfway up to take pictures of the most beautiful scenery in the world. We were looking down at Kathmandu Valley, and all around us were mountains (not too big or overpowering) but – off in the distance, enshrouded by clouds were the snow-capped peaks of the high Himalayas – just shooting up above everything – just spectacular!

As we walked, monkeys were everywhere – big ones (waist high on me), little ones, all of them light brown with red tushies – appearing so human in their actions as to be frightening!

At the top of the hill there's a golden temple called Swayambhunath, into which only monkeys are allowed.

Then we will try for ANOTHER visa extension – we've heard that it's not so easy to get extensions now, because the new king of Nepal is being coronated in February, so the Nepalese govt. wants to clear the city of tourists – especially "freaks." Don't be alarmed by that word – it's just the easiest way to generalize the tremendous amount of young people like myself, who are on the road.

It's amazing how much I am learning and experiencing constantly. This world is so vast – there's just so much life upon it! And I'm really seeing life. At home in Belmont or the surrounding areas, life isn't seen on the streets – people live in houses, work in offices, only using the streets as a medium of getting from one place to another. Here, people are "doing their thing" everywhere – all sorts of street vendors, people making and selling goods, mothers breast-feeding babies, children playing marbles, people eating – you name it – to say nothing of all the animals roaming around – I'm very used to seeing cars stop for cows – ever since Delhi, cows, etc. have been all over the streets. Yes, this part of the world is a bit backwards if compared with Western society. But here, the people seem to be more real. Less of them appear to be robots going to and from – so mechanically. No one here is spoiled by modern conveniences, nothing is wasted. People pick up cow and water buffalo dung, and by mixing it with hay, they use it as fuel for fires. It doesn't smell when burned.

Anyway – yesterday was a really great day – we're trying to convince Roy to come trekking with us, rather than doing the Everest trek as he had planned. The 3 of us get along great – I wish more people from home could be experiencing all that I am – I've only been away 7 weeks and already I have enough stories to tell to last me a lifetime! (If no one hears from me for a few weeks, it's because I'm in the mountains… don't worry – just write again… same address).

 Love,
 Karen

CHAPTER SIX

OUR FIRST TREK!

HELAMBU/LANGTANG REGION OF NEPAL

Monday, December 16

Hello again! Today is Monday, December 16th, and it's hard to believe that I'm looking back on the trek. Such an incredible journey!

Together with Kathy and Jeff, we set out from Kathmandu on Sat. Nov. 30. We caught a bus to a town called Bodhnath, another bus to Sunclarijal, and then we hiked up about 2,000 ft. to Mulkharka where we spent the night with a family. The custom while trekking is to stop at someone's home for dinner, consisting of rice (bat), potatoes (alu), lentils (dal), and if you're lucky, tea, maybe with milk and sugar. We usually paid about 4 rupees (again there are approx. 11 Nepalese rupees to the $1 US), and then we were able to sleep for free.

That first night we slept on the ground floor (don't forget we have our own foam rubber pads and sleeping bags), and the family slept upstairs, as is customary in most Nepalese homes. We were awoken at 6:30 AM by the smoke from the cooking fire – never are there any chimneys – you wouldn't believe the sound of some of the coughs I've heard. From Mulkharka we walked up the 2,000 or so ft. to Patti Bhanjyang which is at about 6,000 ft. Yes, by that time I was very sore – blisters were developing on each toe, and muscles were aching where I hadn't even known they'd existed! At this point David was carrying about 45 lb., and I 30 lb. We went down the 2,000 ft. to Talamarang (3,016) and spent our third night at a dirty place called the Talamarang guest house. Just someone's house with a small store and tea shop out front. However, for breakfast we each had two hard-boiled eggs and chapattis, which are about 6 inches in diameter made of wheat flour and water and then fried (w/o oil). Usually, unless we cooked our own breakfast, the only food available to us was tsampa, which is uncooked chapattis and is served in a big brown lump (not too appetizing looking (or tasting)) with some sort of hot chili sauce. It's pretty difficult to force down, let me tell you. And of course, the Nepalis eat with their hands – we usually used our silverware – unless we were able to wash our hands.

It is now 7:30 AM and I am waiting for my scheduled 8:00 AM hot shower – the first time since Nov. 29! I am amazed at the amount of filth on my body – I scratch my head and my

fingernails come away full of grit. Aaahhhh! But in the mountains I didn't feel so dirty, as it's all natural dirt – no car exhausts, etc.

From Talamarang we climbed 2,600 ft. to the village of Timbu and spent the night. Talamarang marked the beginning of the Helambu region (province), which we spent most of our time in. From Thimbu (5,600 ft.) we climbed (boy was it steep!) up to 8,400 ft. to the pretty large village of Tharke Ghyang. The people there are all sherpas; probably the most intelligent of all the Nepalis. Their homes are bigger, and they have a lot more possessions and food to eat. Sherpas are the people who guide all the big mountain climbing expeditions. They are Buddhists and there's always a "gompa" in each village. Prayer flags hang everywhere and tangas decorate the sides of the building (most Nepalis build with stone, though wood is sometimes used, if it is in abundance). Tangas are brightly painted Buddhist Gods and demons. Usually they're painted on canvas, though the sides of gompas are covered! I'm hoping to find a nice tanga

to bring home. However, some of them are pretty expensive.

In Tharke Ghyang we stayed with a grandmother and her four grandchildren. Their parents had gone to Kathmandu for winter supplies. The oldest child, a 14 yr old girl is becoming a monk, as is her 12 yr. old brother. There's one answer to population control. Anyway, as we were at 8,400 ft., it got pretty damn cold at night, so I put on my black hat with the little flowers. The grandmother LOVED my hat and wanted to trade hers for it. So, I now have a light beige face mask hat – it folds up to look like a cap – and it's one helluva lot warmer than the black one (Not as pretty – but who cares when it's cold!)! We then walked down to 6,200 ft., forded the Melemchi Khola (a river – believe me – it's scary walking across the single log bridges over the rushing water – especially because of the additional 30 lb. I was carrying!)! So, we then climbed back up to 8,400 ft. to the village of Melemchigaon. We were so pooped out, that we spent two nights in Melemchi – recuperating.

And then, on up to Thare Pati (11,900 ft.) which, during this season is nothing but a cluster of shelters. We set up our tents, ate potatoes, turnips, rice, and tea (and biscuits) and watched the sun set over the clouds. Up above the clouds it looked like we were in a plane – but boy was it freezing! We were all bundled up and in our tents by 4:30 PM!

From Thare Pati it was steady climbing to the 15,100 ft. pass over to the sacred lake called Gossainkunda, which is at 14,373 ft. The altitude got to us all quite a bit. David and Jeff developed terrible coughs, none of us were able to sleep (we brought Mandrax sleeping tablets with us, luckily) and air was pretty scarce. At that altitude a higher temperature is needed to boil things so we were using a lot of fuel.

We were up above tree line! We camped at about 14,400 ft. – looking up at the pass. It looked so close, yet the going was REAL rough. It was pretty steep, and because of the altitude, we had to rest every few steps. Finally we reached the top – and suddenly there were the snow-capped peaks of the high Himalaya! Absolutely breathtaking – but it was extremely cold and windy up there, so we hurried on down to the lake – they're frozen solid, but there are really nice stone shelters to stay in. We met up with a group of Americans – actually they all live in India, and go to an American high school in Northern India. They are now on vacation.

Today is a really lousy day; it's rainy and cold – I have so many things to do! I have to go to the American Express office. I have to go to the dentist – I'll go to have my teeth cleaned – dry cleaners is so cheap – 10 cents for one pair of pants – 5 cents a shirt.

CHAPTER SEVEN

HANGING OUT AT THE MONKEY TEMPLE

KATHMANDU

Tuesday, December 17 - 1:00 pm

Hello once again!

At the moment I am awaiting a tossed salad with tuna fish (my 1st salad since Greece!) at an American restaurant in Kathmandu called "The Unity." Today I spent two hours at the American Library catching up on a bit of news. The latest paper was *The Christian Science Monitor* dated Dec. 2. Things are really bad in Israel, continuing to worsen – I'm pretty upset about it and wish more recent news were available.

I also read about Polynesia in the 1974 Dec. *National Geographic*. There are so many places I'm wanting to go! We had been planning to stay in Nepal through January and part of February, heading to Pokhara and trekking to the Annapurna base camp. But the weather is getting pretty lousy.

Yesterday it was raining and really cold, and today is cloudy and raw. So we've decided to head south to Ceylon!

We'll store most of our stuff here in Kathmandu, and will probably come back here in March, just as the rhododendrons are beginning to bloom. Nepal is a really wonderful country, and I would like to spend more

time here. Trekking is an experience everyone should have!

On the trek I learned so much about the basics of life – farming, rice, wheat – how it is prepared for eating. Cows, chicken, yaks, eggs, milk, millet – so much I never knew! The people do EVERYTHING with their hands. Rarely did I see anything machine-made in anyone's home. Because just about all of the country is mountainous, the hillsides must be terraced in order to be used as farmland. The terraces make the hillsides look like giant steps. Each terrace has an upcurved lip to retain the rain water and soil when the monsoons come.

And all is so peaceful in the mountains! The only sounds I heard for 2 weeks (besides us trekking) were the sounds of animals and waterfalls, which are everywhere to be seen! I've been purifying all the water I've had since Greece, but as we walked higher into the mountains and I knew there were no villages above us, I was drinking right out of rivers and streams! I would've loved to wash myself, but you can imagine how cold the water was, as it all flows down from the glaciers. Telling you all everything about trekking will have to wait as it's impossible to write everything.

So now here in Kathmandu, the bustling capital city of Nepal, we are very busy planning our trip south. We must decide what is to come with us and what we'll store here in Kathmandu. And we (especially me) sure do have a lot of crap! We'll probably be traveling with Kathy and Jeff as the four of us get along really well, and it gives us all a chance to spend time with more than just our one partner. Although here in Kathmandu I've been spending time with lots of people; from Toronto, Nova Scotia, all over the states, Australia, New Zealand, England… Dave and I spent the last few days of our trek with 2 really nice Japanese guys. It was so interesting! They are both students (economics) taking a year off and they're just as well equipped as we are. Good sleeping bags, boots, etc. They love to fish and have all sorts of fishing gear with them.

One night the four of us sat sipping tea together in a Nepali home in the town of Beterawaty. They began singing "The Star Spangled Banner" asking us to complete it. And then they sang the Japanese national anthem! One of them had a beautiful sweater on. I asked him where he got it and he said "imported from USA" Apparently – Japan's cost of living is even higher than US!

We've been living like kings in this part of the world, since everything is so cheap. Cornflakes, 2 eggs, 2 pieces buttered toast, and tea cost 4 rupees! And the Chinese and Tibetan food is so good and cheap! It's hard to even imagine things at home…

Yes, there are times when I feel homesick, wishing for a clean bathroom with hot and cold running water, toilet paper in abundance, etc. But I'm constantly learning so much and I realize that the way prices are continually rising all over the world this may be the last chance I'll have to travel, so I'm taking full advantage!

So – as of now our plans are pretty much up in the air as we're heading south – definitely – probably to Ceylon. However, I'm unable to give mailing addresses and know they'll be accurate. The safest thing would be to send mail to Madras – please check and see if there's an Amer. Ex. office in Madras. If not – send it c/o Thomas Cooke and Son (Eng. trav. cheques). I'm now going to see if there's any mail awaiting me at the Amer. Ex. office here in Kathmandu. I miss you and will write more details soon!

Karen

Thursday, December 19 (Happy New Year!)

Nepal is an incredibly beautiful country! The mountains are everywhere, the people are open, smiling and so down-to-earth. We just got back to Kathmandu after trekking for 15 days. We began at 4000 feet and walked up to a 15,100 ft. pass leading to the sacred lake of Gossaindkund at 14,293 feet. Such views of the snow-capped high Himalaya (couldn't see Everest – haven't gone near it – but I love the picture on this card!). It's getting cold here now – time to head south toward Ceylon – and then back to Nepal in the spring for some more trekking. The rhododendron forests will be in bloom, and the sun will be really strong!

Today I walked to the outskirts of Kathmandu to a monkey temple called Swayambhu.

There are monkeys everywhere and some of them are really big.

The temple is really a Buddhist pagoda with monks chanting and

sipping Tibetan tea (tea mixed with yak butter – it's horrid!) Anyway – have good holidays and I hope everyone is well! Mom mentioned you're going to Columbia!? Enjoy! Traveling's great!

Love, Karen

Thursday, December 19 - Noon

Dear Grammy,

Trekking, I lost about 7 pounds. My legs are now solid muscles – no more flabby thighs! Even my stomach has gotten smaller! I spent ¾ of an hour taking in my skirt! A month ago it was 2 ½ inches too big in the waist – today it was 6 inches too big! As I'm sure I've mentioned before, there are a bunch of pie shops offering amazing varieties of delicious pies. I gave one of the bakers your butterscotch brownie recipe and he made them with the exception of the choc. tidbits. I don't know what was missing or what he did wrong, but they just didn't taste right – too much like cake – dry. Oh well – guess I'll have to wait until home for the real thing though with the way prices are rising I may not be able to afford the ingredients! So I'll have you make them, Grammy since you make them the best anyway!

I've spent a lot of time reading and writing. I just finished *The Magus* by John Fowles. I found it really good, though I doubt you would like it very much. Did I ever tell you to read *A Different Woman* by Jane Howard? I really loved it! It's now a paperback on the bestseller list at home.

Back to my plans. We're now in the process of sorting out all our junk, deciding what we'll take with us and what we'll store here in Kathmandu. As we'll be riding trains all the way, and Indian train rides are reputed to be (and from my experience I'll agree) the worst in the world, it's a good idea to travel light. And then after 2-3 months we'll return to Nepal for some more trekking when the rhododendron forests are in bloom.

Trekking is so fantastic! I've learned so much about life – the basics – of how people live off the land using only their own hands, nothing machine-made at all. Sleeping in their homes made of stone with the chickens squawking, roosters crowing at dawn, and the water buffaloes chewing their cud – eating bat and alu (rice and potatoes) every night with tea and maybe a chocolate bar out of my pack for a special treat. Watching the children play marbles, hopscotch, tag – children are the same all over the world! And so often they'd come up to me shouting "Meethi, meethi!" (sweets! sweets!) as other travelers before me have spoiled them with pieces of chocolate or biscuits. So I gave out some of the many Life Savers I had with me.

It amazes me that when my feet would be cold in my thermal socks and hiking boots, and the Nepalis are all barefoot apparently not feeling the cold at all! Their little feet are like leather, as they've been barefoot all their lives, scampering up and down the beautiful Himalayas in which they dwell.

Now I am heading to the monkey temple "Swayambhu." It's a beautiful day – about 50 degrees, blue sky – it's about time!

Love you so much!!!

Karen

(Tell mom my hair is very healthy! Thick and shiny!)

Friday, December 20

Dear Jeri,

It seems like years since I heard from you! In case I didn't tell you, your picture came out beautiful! I have another picture of you with me – the one Debbie took before her trip – of you and I sitting on the living room couch. I miss you!

Let me tell you what it's like to go trekking in Nepal. At first, for 3 or 4 days, I was wondering if it was worth it. I mean, I had 30 pounds of stuff in my pack, and I wasn't at all in shape. All we did all day was CLIMB up and down mountains – for 2 weeks! It doesn't sound like too much fun, does it? But it's great! With each step I could feel all my muscles straining, and my whole body was constantly soaked with sweat. When we were in the lower altitudes we wore shorts. Tell Debbie the dungaree shorts that used to be hers are now way too big for me!

The first night we stayed in a house along with Kathy and Jeff (the two other Americans we were with the whole time), the elderly lady who seemed to be running the house, another woman whom I presume was her daughter,

about ten children of all ages, one man, and tons of chickens who ran around squawking all night. We were each handed a plate, and since no one in the mountains ever uses silverware, the old lady gave us each a huge handful of plain rice. On top she poured a mixture of potatoes and spinach with lots of spice. All the people in the East like their food REALLY spicy. Every bite I take brings tears to my eyes and my mouth burns for about ten minutes. After supper we had some good tea with milk and sugar. Every day for the last 2 months I've had at least two cups of tea! And then, at about 6:30 it was time for bed. The children went crazy over our down (feather) sleeping bags, and kept feeling them and laughing. Finally, they all went upstairs to sleep and us four "tourists" were left alone with the chickens.

Ha ha here's a picture of me resting during a day of trekking:

Early to bed, early to rise… we were awakened by the smoke from the fire (no such thing as stoves or any other fancy stuff) and the sounds of the children laughing and playing. It was only 6:30 AM! Oh well; we got a nice early start. Every night we stayed in a different village from the last meeting different people and learning new things all the time.

As we climbed higher, there were no villages, so we camped. For breakfast we cooked porridge, sometimes using oats, other times flattened rice. We'd put raisins and peanuts in, using sugar or honey… We had brought lots of food with us – peanut butter, soup (powdered), Bournuita (kinda like chocolate), chocolate bars, onions (which we sometimes gave to the women to put in our meals). We had lots of food! For supper we'd cook rice, soup, dal (lentils), and of course we'd have tea. Sometimes we cooked on a fire, but we were so high up in the mountains that we were above treeline! Only little scrubby plants – bushes were everywhere. It looked really strange, like another planet or something. Also we were above the clouds! We watched the sun set OVER the clouds – looking down upon a marshmallow sky – changing from gold to

pink – like from an airplane! It was so cold up there. We had to go to sleep at 4:30!! There were times when we were IN the clouds! It's like thick, thick fog…

And now it's time for me to walk just outside of the city to a place called Swayambhu. There's a steep hill to climb and at the top is a monkey temple! Monkeys everywhere – they really do seem like people! I wish you could be here to see them – and everything else I've seen… Maybe someday you will see them and see Nepal!

I love you and miss you Jeri,
Karen

Sunday, December 21

Dear Mom,

It's 9:30 PM and I sit alone in "The Don't Pass Me By" restaurant. I just read your letter written Dec. 8, the first night of Chanukah! I must admit to not even having known when Chanukah was. For some reason I'm crying.

I guess when I really think about everyone at home – all the family – I realize how much I miss everyone. The two and a half months I've now been on the road seem like 2 1/2 years! So incredibly much has happened. I've been so many places, seen so many different ways of life. And all the time I've been learning about myself. Learning that I am now a mature young woman (getting there, anyway) able to handle herself in a lot of strange situations. I'm learning to listen and to wait. Everything is done at a much slower, much less efficient pace all over the East. I'm becoming a lot more tolerant, and my patience is growing, though there have been times when I've lost my patience (of course I regretted it afterward).

Trekking taught me a lot of things about myself: one thing is that I am capable of climbing up and down steep mountains with 30 lb. on my back, even though at first it seemed impossible. I've grown so strong!

And now we've been back in Kathmandu for a week. It's so difficult to decide where we want to go! I've met people who've been to Indonesia and it sounds like such a tropical paradise… and then there's Kashmir; the most gorgeous handicrafts – rugs especially – come from Kashmir. Nepal is such a wonderful place – I know I'd like to do some more trekking, but it's getting cold, so we're heading south for a while. We're leaving Kathmandu as soon after Xmas as possible.

We've been busy getting ready; I bought some really cheap cotton material for only 7 rupees a meter. It's bright blue with little black and white designs printed. I'm not too fond of it, but it'll do. Anyway, I had baggy, funny looking pajama pants made (only 5 rupees for the tailoring!). They have a drawstring waist and 4 patch pockets and real baggy legs, extremely practical for travel in hot climates. Plus I bought a great big, lightweight blanket for only 25 rupees, which will serve me both as a jacket and blanket. We're planning to travel VERY lightly, storing our parkas, hiking boots, tent and sleeping bags here in Kathmandu until the spring. I've been looking all over town for some sort of large travel bag/shoulder bag. There are bags woven with many different-colored yarns and today I found an ideal bag. It's about 2 1/2 ft. by 3 ft. – my foam rubber pad, blanket, flute, everything would fit in it! But the guy wanted 200 rupees for it. Gradually I got him down to 130 rupees but I refuse to pay more than 100. I'll try again tomorrow.

We're planning to spend a couple of days in Pokhara; I've heard it's very beautiful there. Warmer than Kathmandu where it is cold and very damp at night. From Pokhara we'll go to Lambini, and then down through India – Delhi, Bombay – where I will look up Dr. Shah's family – perhaps they'll be able to put us up. I've heard Bombay is an expensive city. Besides, it would be really interesting to see the way city people (upper class I presume) live.

We've certainly seen mountain people! From Bombay we'll head to Goa, where we'll spend a few weeks. It'll be so nice to stop moving and relax by the ocean in warmth! I feel the need to stop. Here in Kathmandu I've been playing my flute up on the roof of our hotel from which I can see most of the Kathmandu Valley.

It's five stories high. It's nice being in a valley surrounded by small mountains (the foothills to the Himalaya!). And on clear days, the white peaks of the high Himalaya show themselves in the distance. I can even see Swayambhu, which is the section of Kathmandu (a separate village actually) where there is the big monkey temple at the top of a steep hill. Dave, Neil (a guy from San Francisco) and I walked 1/2 way up the hill. I had a bunch of peanuts, some bread, and a few oranges. A cross-eyed monkey came over to us and I was feeding him peanuts. He'd take one by one out of my hand and crack them open; they seem so human! And suddenly we were surrounded by monkeys – about 25 – who fought with each other for the food. It was a bit scary. One big one jumped in my lap to grab the bread from my hand.

So many amazing things happen each day! The whole city is being renovated, or cleaned up because the king is being coronated in February. Believe me, it's pretty dirty here. No proper sewage, animals roaming around, and I do so miss being able to sit down in a bathroom. My legs get tired from squatting on the Eastern style toilets. You probably wouldn't be able to tolerate the filth. But at this point, I'm used to it, and I'm keeping myself as clean as possible. Hot showers are available on order (1 rupee each), I purify all my water – and don't worry about the pies – they're so good and so popular, that as soon as they're baked they're eaten; bacteria doesn't have time to set in!

I plan to do my best looking for a rug for you; I'm honored that you should put trust in my judgment of your bedroom rug! Delhi would probably be my best bet, as it's the safest place from which to ship things home, the most reliable. I'm glad you got the chess set; hope you really do like it. You're very difficult to buy for, you realize. Today I got your letter and I feel closer to you than ever. I'm so glad you write as the road does sometimes get lonely. I love you and it feels good to hear you say you love me and miss me. I feel closest of all to you. I find it a little hard to write home because I'm forced to think of home. And that's a bit scary. Because I still don't know what's there. I've been spending time alone, thinking, and I'm feeling better about myself.

Goodnight – Love, Karen

Monday, December 23 - 8:30 pm

Dear Debbie,

Hey Deb! Happy New Year! The past few times I've heard from Mommy and Grammy, they've mentioned (with pride) that you are directing *The Importance of Being Earnest,* and YOU chose the cast. That's something I wish I'd done. Believe me, there are many things I'm now regretting, kicking myself for, like quitting flute. I won't go into it. You're probably saying "I told you so" in your mind. I really envy you, that you're able to put so much into, and get SO much out of, Belmont High School. That you're able to learn for learning's sake – and when it's distasteful you have the willpower to do it anyway – and always doing it well.

Nepal is beautiful! There are temples, pagodas, prayer flags, statues of Buddha, and

various Hindu gods. Tibetans are beautiful – so strong and proud of genuine coral and turquoise beads, and all Nepalis with their huge earrings and nose rings – the women in this part of the world are gorgeous! People walk around the city selling things; many a person has offered me incredibly adorable Lhasa Apso puppies – some fit in my cupped hands! They're only about $20 or so here – $250 or $300 at Puppy Palace, right? There are some really nice handicrafts here, also! Brightly colored woven shoulder bags, woolen jackets, beautiful Chinese silks – which have their price – silver jewelry – although the silver is not of very good quality. And there are shops selling goods from Kashmir in northern India. If you're not familiar with Kashmiri goods, go into any Indian shop and ask to see some, especially the rugs. They're gorgeous! Mom asked if I would look for a rug for their bedroom (I'm honored that she trusts my taste though the task may prove difficult). Ask her if she likes Kashmiri rugs; there must be some around in Cambridge.

So far I haven't bought much for myself. I had a skirt made in Afghanistan, baggy pajama pants (they're a riot! Bright blue with tiny black and white designs) and are the most practical thing to wear in hot climates since we're heading to southern India next week. We've been without a map most of the way – such a drag without – and today we finally bought a good Bartholomew map of the Indian subcontinent. On December 26 we're heading to Pokhara (the only other city in Nepal) for a few days. Then we'll catch a bus to the border to Gorakhpur. From there we'll catch a train to Agra where I'll see the Taj Mahal. From Agra, hopefully there's an express train directly to Bombay. In Bombay we'll visit Dr. Shah's family, where the little girl (twin sister of the boy with cancer – you know them all from the office) lives – her mother's home. Bombay is an expensive city – maybe we'll be invited to stay. I've written a postcard, "warning" them of my visit. Dr. Shah – the father – may even be there. And then, just as the heat and train rides (the Indian trains are a god-awful nightmare) have gotten us all teased up, we'll reach Goa, where it is possible to rent houses really cheap, living right on the beach!

We have been busy figuring out what is ABSOLUTELY necessary to bring with us. Traveling light is a lot easier – less stuff to worry about having stolen – less to lug around – I'm bringing my pad and a blanket I bought for 20 rupees (11 rps. to $1), flute, First Aid Kit, skirt, bathing suit, p.j. pants, sleeveless leotard, earth shoes – I bought some plastic thongs with soles over an inch thick that keep me cool and a little above the filth that COVERS all Eastern city streets. I haven't been able to sit on a toilet since the bathroom we share at home. And the hot water runs out really quickly, feeling so fine while it lasts.

Lately I've been alone a lot realizing that different backgrounds can mean a lot. David and I are so different. He's a great friend – fun to be with – knows his way in the East, but I can see a definite ending to our relationship. I feel the need to devote myself to one thing – serving humanity. I love children so. Have you ever heard of the Montessori schools? Kathy and Jeff (friends we trekked with) have convinced me I should look into it when I get home though I don't yet know when that will be. I'm taking advantage of where I am and what there is to see in this part of the world. Indonesia sounds great – maybe… who knows when I'll get it together to travel again? Such an amazing education! So kid – congrats on getting your license! My car keys, eh? It sounds like you're happy doing good things. I respect you – wish I could talk to you to tell you how much I've woken up, how much I've learned…

Thursday, December 26 - 1:30 pm

Dear Grammy,

The last two days we've spent our time partying – using X-mas as our excuse. On the 24th we splurged and went out for a fantastic turkey dinner at "Aunt Jane's" restaurant. Turkey, stuffing, cauliflower, gravy, carrots, salad, and coffee – 24 rupees – sounds cheap to you as it's less than $2.40, but for this part of the world and for the way we've been living it's a real lot of money to spend for one meal. But it was good, even though there wasn't any cranberry sauce, dessert, or second helpings.

Later that night (our meal was at 3:00 PM), we got together with friends in our hotel room. Neil, from San Francisco, Jim from Los Angeles, Kathy and Jeff (Ohio) with whom we've spent lots of time and have become pretty close. Also, Joe and Retla, a really nice couple from Tasmania, New Zealand. We cooked grilled cheese sandwiches with a tomato, onion, garlic sauce. Then we made garlic butter and put it on toasted French bread. Neil made an incredible "Keere" – Indian rice pudding. First he boiled some milk – about a quart – then added the rice, some sugar, raisins, dates, FRESHLY dried coconut, and raw cashews! Such a treat! And of course we had oranges (mandarins) and tea. It was so nice to cook ourselves – so much fun being with friends we've known for a while – been traveling with off and on. As restaurants here serve such good food so cheaply, we've been eating out constantly. Last night we went to a little cold drink store called "The Mandala."

We decorated a juniper tree with balloons, cut paper stars, lights and a Dutch man named Ton made up a delicious fruit salad including mandarins, apples, raisins, cashews, and spices! Cinnamon, anise, cardamom, with whipped cream mixed with yogurt on top! There's delicious yogurt here in Kathmandu – so naturally sweet that no fruit or sweetening is necessary! And there was wine in the salad also.

And you must be wondering how I am. I'm feeling really fine – though a little bit overweight – I'm sure I'll lose weight when I'm traveling as fast as possible through India – 2,500 miles to Goa from here… We're going to start moving southward tomorrow. At 7:00 AM, tomorrow, we're taking a bus to Pokhara (6 hours away), Nepal's only other city. I'm really excited. Pokhara is lots warmer than Kathmandu I hear. Here in Kathmandu I've had to wear my down parka as soon as the sun goes down. There's a beautiful lake there, and tremendous mountain range called the "Annapurnas" (Annapurna itself is at 26,795 ft. high!) only 25 miles away. They must be incredible. Our trek in the Himalayas didn't take us very close to any of the high Himalaya. We got a few fantastic views – but always of fairly far away peaks – actually did get close (2 miles) away from Lantang I and II – 22,000 and 23,000 ft. But we were looking at them from an altitude of 15,100 ft – Pokhara is only at 2,900 ft., so Annapurna should look massive.

I'm looking forward to spending some time in warm, swimming weather by the ocean. I'm a little tired of constantly moving though I'm not at all tired of traveling. This world really is incredible. Things are SO DIFFERENT in this part of the world. Europe has basically the same "rate" of living as the US, but as one goes East – Greece begins the strangeness – Turkey – Afghanistan seems like it's 250 years behind the rest of the world, and here in Nepal everything is timeless, ageless. I'm learning so much, meeting so many interesting people; many, many fellow travelers. There are so many westerners here in Nepal, that the whole city celebrated X-mas – but no religious significance was around – only decorations. It's fun to celebrate something rather than just have a party.

Hope you're well – miss you and love you
– Karen

CHAPTER EIGHT

HAPPY NEW YEAR 1975!

POKHARA, NEPAL

Monday, December 30 - 7:30 am

Dear Mom, Dad, Deb, Jeri, Grammy,

Things are constantly changing along the traveling road. Friday morning we caught a 7:00 AM bus to Pokhara. It should have taken only 5 hours, but the brakes failed, causing quite a delay; we didn't reach Pokhara until 8:30 PM! Anyway, as it was dark when we arrived, it was an amazing thrill to see the REAL big Himalaya so near. Machapuchure is the most beautiful mountain (22,000 ft.) – the way its peak rises so steeply into a point. Find a picture – in English, "Machapachure" means "fish-tail"). And the whole Annapurna mass can be seen from all over the valley. They're about 30 miles away, but since Pokhara's only at 2,900 ft. and they're well over 20,000 ft each, they're awesome and look much closer.

In the daytime the sun shines (there are a few clouds) constantly, and it must be about 75-80 degrees in the sun. The lake is really beautiful – I may even go for a swim! I'm definitely planning to rent a boat.

A boy asked us if we'd like to rent a house for 25 rupees a week. So we took a look and fell in love with it – and here I am now! I guess there are houses everywhere around for rent, as so many children ask us where we're going and want us to go with them.

Our house is made of sun-baked orange-colored mud (clay). We live upstairs as there are 4 large windows, the door and another door leading to a great balcony from which we could see the full moon illuminating the snow-capped peaks. Most houses we've seen have very small windows, which let in hardly any light. I find them a bit depressing, but here tons of sunlight gets in, and there's even electricity, one light bulb! In the house there are two wooden beds though no mattresses or anything. Two tables with some framed photos of the boy's family. I guess the 16 yr. old boy who showed us here

lives here and his family lives right next door. There's no fireplace upstairs, which is just as well, considering we have a good little stove – a fire would fill the house with smoke. For some reason the Nepalis never use any sort of chimney, and the smoke is usually unbelievably thick.

Our house is about a ten minute walk to the lake. Outside there's a water faucet, which has supposedly clean drinkable water, available only from 6:00-8:00 am and again from 5:00-7:00 pm (I'm purifying it anyway). Yesterday we walked the 40 minutes into the main bazaar to buy some food. We're really saving money living this way instead of out of hotels and restaurants.

This place is incredibly peaceful – birds everywhere, butterflies, cows, goats, chickens, ducks, water buffalo, and the vegetation looks almost tropical – there's so much green! Tremendous banyan trees, banana trees, papaya trees, poinsettia trees. The bright red looks so beautiful against all the green. Ferns, little yellow flowers, it really is incredible, such a utopia! The toilet consists of a big hole in the ground with logs to stand on, sheltered by a fence of shrubbery.

Hope all is well – love everyone!
Karen

Saturday, January 4 - 11:00 am

Hello! Today is a really gorgeous day – about 75 and clear, whereas the past few days have been pretty cloudy, with a big rain storm both last night and 3 nights ago. I guess there was a lot of rain (most of it was when I was sleeping) – because the huge concrete dam at the end of the lake got a big hole in it, and then over half of it fell away, leaving all of Pokhara Valley without electricity, and the lake is rapidly draining away. It's been 3 days, and it's gone down over 25 ft. The lake is 4 miles long and 1/2 mile wide! As I've told you, our house is right near the lake, and we have (had) electricity.

Oh well, it was convenient having a light to cook by. I've been cooking a lot lately as there are many vegetables and spices available, and we have the stove (which runs on regular car gas) and pans. Every morning, a fresh loaf of bread is delivered to our door by a man on a bicycle, another woman brings us eggs, and a man comes around with fresh milk (which we boil for 20 minutes). I'm having such a great time. I was getting tired of living out of my pack constantly and always having so much crap to lug around. Now I have only my small army knapsack and a fairly large bag I picked up in Kathmandu. Our packs are stored in Kathmandu for when we return to trek after the king's coronation. With me I have my foam pad, a blanket which serves as both jacket and for sleeping, my cotton skirt from Afghanistan, my pajama pants, my sleeveless leotard, tights, knee socks, underwear, earth shoes, thongs (with 2 1/2" sole to keep my above dirty city streets), my long john shirt, and of course the First Aid kit, soap, etc. It's really nice to have a place for everything, and to be in one place for a little while.

I've been getting to know the villagers – every morning I wait in line to fill my water container. Never do I have to wait long because the women always fill my container before their own – they're so friendly, always helping me out. And whenever we're cooking, 4 or 5 children come to watch.

I realize that my recent letters have sounded very disjointed and indecisive. I apologize for not being able to give you any exact dates and for the fact that we keep changing our minds, but this seems to be the way of the traveling road – every day finding out new things about different places, new ideas of places to visit – new people sharing different stories.

Last night we were sitting in a restaurant (it was raining out) and an American guy was playing folk songs on the guitar, so I joined him on my flute. I've been playing a lot lately – even getting back into reading some music (we have 2 books with us)! I regret having ever quit playing – as I regret many other things I shunned for my various immature reasons. But those days are behind me, and now I'm learning all that I can. My Nepali is improving daily, I'm taking long walks every day – sometimes into town, or to the Tibetan refugee camp an hour or so away from here – there are many Tibetan traders roaming around, selling beautiful pieces of coral and turquoise. I've learned quite a bit about their quality and today (2 minutes ago!) I bought two really pretty coral beads for 7 rupees each, and I put one on each of my plain hoop earrings. I'm hoping to buy more so cheaply!

My health has been excellent – the cold I caught while trekking has finally gone – now that we've been in the sun for a week I wish so much that you all could be here – that you could see and experience all that I am – this is quite an education! Unfortunately, there's probably mail for me in Kathmandu which I won't receive for many months, but I look forward to hearing from you all when I get to Bombay and Goa!

Love, Karen

Tuesday, January 7

Dear Grammy,

I've been traveling for 3 months now – sometimes it seems more like 3 years. I've been in so many places, met so many people, learned so very much about the world we live in. But then again, it also feels like only 3 days ago that I said "good-bye" to you and everyone else. Today we climbed the 2,000 ft. hill (tiny mountain compared to the high Himalaya shooting far above all else) from the top was the most spectacular view I've ever seen – probably the best in the world – just 25 miles away – beyond the valley with a lovely river running through and the thatched roofed orange clay houses.

Before me lay some of the highest mountains in the world – Annapurna massive consisting of 6 mountains all over 25,000 ft. and Machapachure ("macha" means fish and "pachure" means tail) 22,925(?) it's a really beautiful mountain, the way it juts out – all rocks and snow and ice – so much mountain! So overpowering. And the blue bluer than anywhere in the world – and the plush green terraced hillsides – Oh how I wish you could see it – and I could see you.

I miss you – and knowing that you're thinking of me and loving me, and I want you to know that you are on my mind a real lot – that I feel sad that I can't speak with you and be with you – but I know that I should be taking advantage of the fact that I'm on the road now – who knows if and when I'll be able to travel again? It's the best education the world has to offer and I'm loving it! There are so many places I'd like to see – after staying in Goa for a little while we're returning to Nepal (maybe we'll go down to Sri Lanka, I don't know yet). And after Nepal it'd be nice to go to Indonesia – many people tell me about its being a utopia tropical paradise – really cheap – and then there's Greece – so much in this world to see!

Saturday, January 11

Namaste!

I know you all must be wondering what it's really like here, so for the past couple of days I've been taking pictures, and I plan to send this roll home from India. The first 5 or 6 pictures were taken from the top of the 2,000 ft. hill overview! The entire Annapurna massive consisting of 6 separate peaks all over 24,000 ft. and there's "Machapachure" (Fishtail), my favorite mountain – David took a picture of me with it behind. And there's a few shots of Nepali children – one 10 yr. old girl named Harigaly (roll

the "r") to whom I gave a pen – children always ask for pens! Nepali people are really beautiful. So of course I took lots of pictures for you to see – especially of children. It amazes me how primitive life is here, compared to the western world. The people work really hard – little children are able to carry amazing loads – as are all Nepalis. A large basket with a strap is used, the strap worn around the forehead so all the weight is felt in the neck muscles! This is also the way sherpas and porters carry supplies for expeditions.

Have I ever mentioned the fact that all the children in the East (here anyway) are bare-bottomed until the age of 3 or 4? Saves on diapers anyway! And the women all have long, long hair, worn in one braid, and their jewelry is amazing! Gold rings in their noses – some women have up to 10 earrings in each ear! And beautiful strings of coral and turquoise around their necks! Many Tibetan guys (traders) are around selling old handicrafts: brass cups, knives, beautiful coral and turquoise. I've bought 4 small coral beads. Two of them are fine quality – I've also bought one little piece of turquoise that is not particularly fine quality, but it's really pretty. I'm hoping to buy some more if I'm able to get a good price.

Back to the pictures – I took quite a few pictures of the mountains – no matter how long I've been here, the mountains still overwhelm me – they're just so big and white and powerful! Also, I took lots of pictures of the village – houses, people, water buffaloes – it really is beautiful here!

Tuesday, January 14 – 10:00 pm

Dear Grammy,

Today was a Hindu festival day held in honor of the Goddess Sita's return to the earth (supposedly the earth opened up…). It's described in detail in one of the major Hindu epics, "Ramayana." Sita was the wife of Rama – sorry I can't tell you the story – it's too complicated to write and I know it only vaguely. Anyway – there was a big fair held about 1 1/2 hour walk from our house. We had no problem finding it, as the streets were filled with people all dressed up – brightly-colored saris, amazing jewelry, and many, many people came down from the hills – many carrying tremendous baskets (which they carry on their backs, held on by a strip worn around the forehead) filled with vegetables: turnips, spinach, cauliflower (I've made some terrific meals using cauliflower!) …

And the festival – I had expected lots of singing and dancing – hoping to see people wearing all sorts of costumes, etc. But we were a bit disappointed as all we saw were thousands of Nepalis – many, many little stands selling veggies, straw mats, and bamboo woven into large pizza sized patterns used by the people to shake grains like rice – a sifter actually. And colorful plastic bangle bracelets (6 for a rupee) worn by most women and girls, and weird assortments of "western" goods, like a blanket laid upon the ground with a few bottles of nail polish, cigarette lighters, rubber balls, snaps, pens, plastic dolls, rubber thongs which seem to be the only shoes ever worn by most Nepalis (if they wear any at all), big baskets filled with mandarin oranges (5 for a rupee) and sweets, tea stands – the thing everyone's supposed to

eat on this holiday is sugar cane! 6-foot stalks sold for 50 paisa (less than 5 cents), an inch (give or take a little) in diameter. It tastes so good! First it must be skinned – it looks like thin bamboo – and then cut and chewed – it's so refreshing – sweet, white and hard – after all the juice has been sucked out you spit out the pulp.

After a little while we got bored and headed with our Australian friend, Bob, to the room he rents in a Tibetan refugee camp another 1/2 hour or so away. The walk over was through fields all terraced even on flat land – so the monsoon rains won't wash them away. Mustard seed fields with bright yellow flowers and monkeys scampering about the amazing white peaks of the high Himalaya, which overwhelm all else…

The refugee camp consists of about 10 long white buildings – long rows of attached houses where about 300 Tibetans live. They're from all over Tibet – many of them don't even

know from where! Tibetan people really resemble American Indians – they're brown-skinned with high cheekbones, slanted eyes, the women wear their long, long hair in braids and beautiful turquoise and coral jewelry.

We were sitting in Bob's room – he's an amazing guy – has a 9 inch, full, sand-colored beard, huge green eyes and he's studying the Tibetan language and planning to go to Lhasa (the capital). He'll have to sneak over the border! Sounds really exciting, but something I'd certainly be scared to do!

While we were there, a Nepali official came and told Bob he'd have to leave because 150 refugees were coming today, and as it is, there is a shortage of housing. The new arrivals are from Mustang (I read *Mustang, The Forbidden Kingdom* by Michel Peissel – I think you'd like it), and were supposedly prisoners of war – there's lots of Khampa warriors that are Tibetans who are wanting revenge from the Chinese for taking their land away in 1962 – and various treks have been closed, due to guerrilla warfare along the border! So 150 more Tibetans wanting to practice their religion freely and unable to under the Chinese government have come to Nepal – and the Nepalese government made them come without even their personal things! I've walked by them and it was quite an experience. I'm used to seeing Nepalis who are all very small and I always feel so huge. Most of the Tibetans I've seen before today also have been small – but these people were something else! The men are about 6' with broad Chinese-looking faces, are mostly western-dressed (not the latest styles, believe me), many wearing glasses and all staring at us as though we'd jumped off the moon!

The coolest thing was the Tibetan monk I ran into. He was wearing robes and counting his mala beads held behind his back as he walked, chanting. Fascinated, I simply stood in the middle of the path as he walked straight toward me. As he came up to me and I stood my ground he looked up from his walking meditation and saw me, clearly not looking like anyone he'd ever seen before. He continued his chanting but his voice rose and his eyes widened and he chanted a bit faster and louder before walking around me. I was the first westerner he'd ever encountered.

    Love,
    Karen

CHAPTER NINE

A LAND OF CONTRASTS

AGRA AND THE TAJ MAHAL

Wednesday, January 22

Dear everyone,

We arrived here in Agra yesterday morning at 6:30. I would have written sooner if I'd had anything to write upon – plus being in transit makes it very difficult. We left Pokhara on Friday morning and took a bus to the border. There were 10 other westerners on our bus – an English couple, a French guy, and 7 Australians. The 12 of us took a mini bus from Sunauli, the border town, to Gorakhpur, 3 hours away. There's no direct train to Agra from there, so Dave and I had to change trains in Lucknow. Our train left at 1:00 PM Sat. the 18th (together with the English couple and 3 Aus. guys we stayed in a dormitory room in a nearby hotel). Reservations were booked up for several days, so we ended up riding II class, unreserved. The train was really crowded as only Indian train rides can be, and as it grew dark, my bag was stolen (the small green knapsack). *(See entire story in intro.)* Fortunately, my passport, travelers' cheques, address book, Swiss knife, plane ticket, etc. I always wear in a pouch around my neck and under my shirt.

The next day we went to the railway police and spent 5 hours filling out forms in hopes of them helping us find the thief. What the heck were we thinking? There are 621 million people in India!

12 copies had to be made – who knows why – good old Indian bureaucracy. I tried to get them to arrange us to travel 1st class (which is ridiculously expensive) and they said yes it could be arranged for the 9:00 PM train and that we should return to the station at 8:00. Of course they couldn't swing it – they offered us an armed guard, but I simply wasn't into it… too traumatized.

And then we said the hell with them all – they weren't going to help us – and then we ran into Sharon and Martin (the English couple I mentioned) – boy was I happy to see a familiar western face! We'd thought they'd gone to Delhi, but as is to be expected, they also had train (ticket purchasing) problems and they had also been stuck in Nepal. So Dave and I talked to the man in charge of Reservations (the first kind, understanding, INTELLIGENT person we'd come across) and he crossed off someone else's reservation and gave us the upper berths in the II class reserved 3-tiered sleeper car with bars on the windows. No one without a reservation is even allowed in the compartment. So the four of us headed back to our hotel where we spent the evening discussing all our various Indian bureaucratic "episodes." Amazing how healing empathy can be!

The next night (Monday), we settled ourselves upon our upper berths, said a teary goodbye to Sharon and Martin (who could possibly be coming to Boston within the year), and off we went to Agra.

And here I sit now, in a little tea shop with Dave and Ishwa, a really nice bicycle rickshaw driver, sipping tea and waiting for my hard-boiled eggs. We're staying at the "Bengal Lodge Hotel" where we have a nice big room with two beds, table, chairs, vanity and attached toilet and water faucet. Yesterday we went into tons of tourist shops (this is such a tourist town!) that look exactly like the Indian shops at home! Ishwa asked us to please go in to look in the real expensive shops, as he gets a 50 paisa tip every time he brings prospective customers around. We were more than willing to help him out.

And now – Ishwa is going to take us to the Taj Mahal – it's hard to believe I'm really going to see one of the seven wonders of the world! And now Ishwa is peddling us to the post office so I can mail this home – you must be worried – the last time I wrote was Friday the 17th and I mailed it from the border.

Today I'm going to buy a skirt and David's going to pick up the beautiful ring he's having made. Silver encasement with a black star stone. I will write again tonight – I want this to get home – we have reservations for the 25-hour train to Bombay – leaves at midnight the 24th – I wrote again to Dr. Shah's mother – hope we'll be able to stay there.

Love you All! Miss you!   Karen

Wednesday, January 22

Hello everyone,

India really is a land of extremes. Agra is considered a small city with only 250,000 people and it's spread out, so the streets aren't quite as crowded as they are in most Indian cities. We're staying in a hotel situated about 15 minutes (by bicycle rickshaw) from the Taj Mahal, which is everything I've heard and more.

This morning, we went to a little tea shop around the corner where we'd told our rickshaw driver we'd meet him. He's 26 years old and has driven or should I say, peddled a bicycle rickshaw in Agra for the past five years. Before that he'd lived in a village outside of Delhi until his wife died. He lives in the small, windowless garage of a wealthy Sikh. Ishwar Singh is a really good, honest man. He speaks English well, as Agra is quite a tourist town. Mom, you would love some of the bright patterns like the pattern on the dress you and I each have. There are beautiful silks, cotton-silk mixtures, velvety wool shawls with intricate embroideries, scarves, skirts, shirts, saris… they really are pretty and I look good in them. I'm considering buying one, except they would probably be a pain in the neck on trains, etc. There are so many materials to choose from and I'm having a real tough time making a decision! Besides clothing, Agra is full of marble – miniature Taj's, tables, boxes – it's all quite beautiful, but I'm not interested in buying any that I don't need. My money is rapidly dwindling – even though everything's 10 times cheaper than home, those rupees do begin to add up.

Did you receive my letter (written this morning) in which I mentioned the fact that my bag was stolen? We were riding the train from Gorakhpur to Lucknow, where we would change trains for Agra. But, I did lose a few things such as my diary. I can't believe it's gone! So much of me went into that diary; so many thoughts, feelings. My whole trip thus far recorded including the addresses of people I've met along the way and pictures of different things such as food labels and photos cut out of tourist brochures. In Pokhara I had picked lots of pretty little flowers, dried them and made some nice arrangements. That diary was great because it closed and had a lock and key and the pages were bigger than this piece of paper. Oh well, it's fate I guess, and though it was very difficult to accept at first I have no choice. It's gone. It was traumatizing that someone actually robbed me… but at least I wasn't hurt and David was with me. But that happened on Saturday night, the 18th, and now it's Wednesday night the 24th and so much has happened in between it seems like a long time ago.

As I said, India is a land of extremes. One minute my bag gets stolen, and the next minute (actually 3 days later), I'm at the Taj Mahal.

I can't believe how gorgeous it really is with all the gardens and fountains. From the grand archway of an entrance half a kilometer from the Taj itself, I was filled with a sense of awe. Everything is built and/or painted symmetrically, down to each bush or little flowering tree. As I walked closer I could see the beautiful stone inlays of jade, rubies, amber, etc., all set in intricate designs mostly in flower patterns – each perfectly rendered. And inside, precisely in the center, is the tomb of Shah Jahan's second and most beloved wife, Momtaj Mahal, in whose memory the Taj was built. And just to the left of her tomb is the Shah's tomb. We took some really good shots with the wide-angle lens (glad we have a good camera because a Kodak instamatic sure wouldn't do the Taj much justice!)

Wednesday, January 24 – 4:00 pm

Dear Jeri,

It's 4:00 PM now and I'm sitting on the roof of our hotel. It's a beautiful day – about 65 degrees and crisp. The "Bengal Lodge Hotel" is located on a relatively quiet street (Indian streets are always much noisier than Bright Road – or anywhere else in the world except maybe China).

Ten cute little donkeys walked by with bells around their necks and tremendous loads of turnips, cement blocks – you name it and donkeys carry it around – and yesterday I saw a really big camel cruising down the street with a load of carpets – they are incredibly ugly creatures! Oh – another bunch of donkeys just walked by – this time they had no loads (a little boy was riding one and keeping the others in line) and each donkey had a rope tied from its right to left ankles – it doesn't hurt them – just prevents them from running away. And here comes two Sikhs, riding a motorcycle! Sikhs are upper class, educated Indians. The men wear various colored turbans covering the hair they've never cut in their lives, and hair nets over their beards holding them tightly to the face. I'm sorry I can't explain why, but it is forbidden in the Sikh religion for men to cut their hair or shave. They're very regal looking – dark skin, handsome faces, sharply dressed (western style).

And there goes a little herd of goats; the baby ones are so adorable!

There are bicycle rickshaws everywhere – they're the most common form of transportation here – and cheapest. A mile ride costs us only about 7 cents! There are horse-drawn

taxis around and big lorries – that's the English (British) word for trucks; because England controlled India for so long, many signs are written in English and Hindi – and everyone speaks English (it's difficult for me to understand educated Indians speaking English because they speak it with British accents on top of their Hindi accents!)

This street really is interesting – I keep getting distracted from writing! Here comes another bunch of donkeys, and a herd of sheep, and a wooden cart hauled by two men just went by – the cart was stacked high with patties of cow and water buffalo crap – when dried it doesn't smell and believe it or not, it burns very well, providing cheap fuel for cooking and heating. Wood is hard to find and expensive in the cities, and there's crap all over the streets because animals are everywhere – and you know that in the Hindu religion cows are considered to be holy, and they're free to roam all over the city streets. Traffic must go around them or stop. When the Indians walk by them, they touch the cows' heads for good luck.

And here comes a typical Indian bus packed with about 200 people – no exaggeration! Indians are all very small, and because this country is so amazingly crowded they're all used to being in crowds – I've seen as many as 7 people sharing 2 seats on a train! The steering wheels are on the right and driving is done on the left side of the road, just like in England.

But India is also full of wonderful things such as beautiful temples, and arts and crafts to tempt me everywhere I go. Here in Agra, there's the Taj Mahal, which has got to be the most beautiful building in the world! And as you can tell by all the things I'm watching go by in the street below, that India is fascinating – so very different than home!

Love,
Karen

CHAPTER TEN

BOMBAY AND MY NEW JOURNAL!

BOMBAY

Monday, January 27

Dear Grammy,

It's hard to believe that at this very moment I am sunning myself on the beach of the Arabian Sea. Behind me lies the huge bustling city of Bombay, and it stretches up the palm-tree lined coast as far as I can see in either direction. Directly behind me there are 4 or 5 very ritzy hotels – $50 a night – Bombay is very expensive compared to the rest of India. I'm so glad we're staying with Dad's patients' relatives! They're so kind – really giving us the red-carpet treatment – making us feel so at home! You know what just happened? A tremendous camel with a man sitting on its back just lumbered up to our blanket, and we were offered a camel ride! For a small fee, of course. About 15 minutes ago, we were offered horse-back rides. Everything is sold around here! In Agra, a man massaged David's head for a rupee, and a friend of ours from Georgia had a manicure and foot massage for 50 paisa.

On the trains, men and boys are constantly walking through the cars selling peanuts, chai tea, coca cola, bananas, balloons, toys, books (English and/or Hindi), newspapers, magazines, salads made on the spot (I stay away from them – and all other food that's raw and undoubtedly unwashed).

11:15 pm

And now I am sitting upon the mattress that's been provided for me in the living room of Dr. Shah's mother and sister's apartment. Two-year-old Roopah (roll the "R") is sitting with me – she's just as cute as can be – olive-skinned, dark eyes, short, wavy, almost black hair, little gold hoops in her ears, and she's wearing a lavender and white polka dotted dress. I should explain that Roopah is the daughter of Dad's Indian patients who live in Lexington. Before our trip they invited Dave and me to dinner and told us

we'd be welcomed in Bombay to stay with their family. They have four children: girls ages 6 and 4 and 2-year-old boy and girl twins – a boy and a girl. The little boy has Leukemia so naturally requires tons of attention. His twin, Roopah, was sent here to Bombay to stay with the elderly grandmother and unmarried auntie. They consider it a win-win in that Roopah will get tons of attention and the ladies won't be so lonely.

It's too bad she's so spoiled although it really can't be helped, as she's the only child around, totally surrounded by adults. She speaks quite a bit, but unfortunately, she knows only the family's native tongue of Gujarati, which is a dialect of Hindi. So I'm unable to speak with her. But her aunt, Dr. Shah's sister, Dhana, a school teacher, speaks English very well, as she's spent a total of 4 years in the states, where she studied at Long Island University. I imagine I'll teach Roopah some English while I'm here!

January 28 – 9:30 am

And now I'm sipping a delicious cup of ginger milk tea – and in a minute Dhana is going to make us some Aunt Jemima's pancakes with honey. No such thing as maple syrup in India as far as I can tell! Dr. Shah was here only two or three weeks ago and he bought all sorts of all-American foods with him, like the pancake mix, Chef Boyardee pizzas, cereal, Nestle's strawberry Nesquik, Coffeemate, A+P powdered nutmeg and cinnamon – it's funny to see all these very familiar foods on the shelves, as I haven't seen anything American for quite a while!

As I've said before and will say a hundred times again – India is a land of extremes. Here in Bombay the streets are filled with cars – most of them small European models with steering wheels on the right-hand side as of course driving is done on the left side of the road – just like in England. Although I've been here (Nepal also – driving is done on the left side) a while, I'm still not used to this "wrong" side of the road business. I have to be very careful when crossing the street to look in the right direction!

Also, there are a few American cars around which are so big compared to the European

models. And of course cars aren't the only vehicles on the roads. Many, many people ride bicycles, motorcycles and scooters. I've seen whole families on them. Mother, Father, and two or three children all on one scooter! Horse drawn carts, huge Brahma bulls pulling heavy loads of bricks or vegetables – anything you can think of – tremendous lorries gaily painted and decorated, buses everywhere – a lot of them are double-deckers like in England – there are so many people in this country that the buses should be quadruple-deckered!

Bombay is really modern – some young women wear mini-skirts which came as a shock as I haven't seen a miniskirt since we were in Austria! Little brown-skinned children are everywhere playing marbles, or working. There certainly don't seem to be any laws against child labor here in India. I've seen children as young as 5 or so working in restaurants, shining shoes, selling peanuts, begging. I hear it's like Fagan's gang where children are taught to beg as soon as they're able to talk!

The caste system was supposedly abolished two years ago – but believe me, it seems to still very much exist. It's obvious who the upper class are. The women are usually fat and wearing beautiful silk saris. Then there's the low classes consisting of masses of dirty, straggly-haired, rag-bedecked, skinny people who are everywhere, many diseased and begging. It's very sad… This country really seems full of problems: earthquakes, famines, floods, droughts… Here in Bombay the water supply is apparently limited, as monsoon rains haven't come for the last two years. I've heard about many riots and assassinations – you name it!

But there are good and beautiful things in India as well; definitely a country of contrasts!

Today we're going into the city to see some museums and to walk around this amazing metropolis.

Bombay is India's film center, so everywhere there are billboards, advertising movies and cinemas. Big modern buildings are everywhere! And the English influence is very apparent here: lots of English architecture, tremendous churches, etc. And English is spoken everywhere with more signs in English than Hindi. Indians speak in English with one another, which makes it easy for me to make my needs known!

How've you been lately Grammy? I had hoped there'd be a letter from you here in Bombay – but there was only one beautiful letter from Mom. I should've told you to write here – but I'll be in Goa soon enough. Last night I ordered prescription sunglasses – only

60 rupees and my other ones cost me over $60 at home! My health is really good, except that I'm gaining weight – it's very difficult with all the starches, and our kind hostess insists we eat so much – at least three helpings! In Goa I'll be preparing my own food, so I'll try and lose weight. Anyway – here are my pancakes!

Know that I love you and please write!
Karen

(Journal) February 1, 1975

Now I begin the third diary of my journey, having lost the other two. It's impossible to re-record thoughts and experiences that happened between October the 6th when I first left home, and today – February the 1st, 1975. At least I wrote a lot of letters home to everyone, which I hope they'll keep!

I can't believe that in five days it'll be four full months that we've been on the road! It really has gone by quickly – seems like yesterday that I looked through millions of tears, back at #67 Bright Rd. and Dad standing on the front steps, arm outstretched, reaching for me, and I know there were tears in his eyes also…

And now we, Dave and I, are staying at the home (apt.) of Dr. Shah's sister Dhanalaxshmi, his daughter (2 yr. 2 mos.), and his mother. It feels really good to have a place we can call home, even if it is only temporary. Just as I've always heard, Indian people are amazingly hospitable. We've been getting red carpet treatment since Monday morning when we arrived. The Goradia's are Gujarati, which is one of India's 22 main languages. Dhana speaks fluent English, as she's spent a total of four years in the states, studying and then visiting the Shah's. But little Roopa, who's just adorable but spoiled to the degree that I (and David) find it difficult to tolerate. Anyway – she speaks only Gujarati – as does the Grandma. I can't understand anything they say. Gujarati sure sounds different from Hindi!

But Gujarati cooking is the best of Indian cooking as far as I'm concerned. Amazing meals are prepared for us by all the relatives, and everyone wants us to eat at their home. Of course chilies are used, but not to the degree that their potency overrides the other spices, such as mustard seeds, cardamom, ginger, molasses. Gujarati food is sort of sweet and spicy – mmmmm.

Today we went into the city to meet Cathy and Steve – I hope we'll all get a house together, but I don't know when they'll make it to Colva Beach. We're heading there immediately. Together we went to the silver bazaar in a really crowded section of town, like Old Delhi. There were hundreds of beggars. Some of them were in REALLY sad shape, lots of lepers here in Bombay, and a man came up to us and exposed the most revolting-looking hernia. His guts were literally spilling out, and he kept them in a sack hanging from his waist. I'll never be able to harden completely… I've found that the easiest way is to not make any eye-contact. It really is pitiful, but what can I do?

India certainly is FULL of sad things – 621,000,000 people. It's hard to believe until you see all the skinny, dark-skinned, dirty rag-bedecked people and the shacks (not even!) that line the streets and all the railway tracks… Everywhere one looks there is human habitation in all forms!

(Journal) Monday, February 3

It's hard to believe that we're actually heading to Goa this afternoon! It'll be nice to relax by the sea, to get into myself. That's what I need more than anything: to gather my thoughts together. Four months on the road and I feel like I really haven't come very far regarding my own self reliance.. It's been too easy to lean on David. He's been on the road before and knows the ins and outs regarding where to go, etc. I must make my own decisions! Karen – stop listening to others all the time, damn it, what's the matter with you? You have a good head – why don't you use it more often? Enough lecturing to myself– I'm making a promise to myself to try harder; I will keep my head up, and if something goes wrong, I'll do my best not to smear my worries on anyone else. David really has put up with a LOT of shit from me, hasn't he?

Dhana has been so kind! She's even invited us to stay here when we return to Bombay after Goa in five weeks or whenever! And it's fine for us to leave as much crap as we wish to, right here. I wish we were traveling even lighter than we are, but we are carrying things to make a comfortable home, so I shouldn't complain. Time to go get my shit together!

Monday, February 3

Dear Grammy,

This afternoon we are taking a bus to Goa – it leaves at 5:00 pm and arrives tomorrow morning at 10:00. Dr. Shah's sister has been so nice and hospitable. We just finished a delicious lunch of dal (lentils) soup, chapattis, a curried cabbage and peas mixture, greens cooked with chilies – tasted just like spinach but it's called something else. I'm finally becoming accustomed to hot, spicy food – and I love it, providing the chilies don't override all else!

I finally received your letter dated December 15 along with letters from Mom, Dad, Jeri, Linda Jefferson and Gail. We'd asked American Express in Kathmandu to forward my mail here to Bombay; I'm shocked that they actually did so! It felt great hearing from everyone – it was the first letter I've received from Linda J. and also from Gail. They're both doing well in college and seem quite happy.

In your letter you said reading my letters makes you sad – especially when I talk about all the "freaks" I'm meeting. I'm sorry I've used that word. It's just that there are so many young people like us on the road, from every country you can think of, and it makes it easier to categorize them with one word rather than saying "all the young people traveling" every time.

Of course there are many people who've been traveling for years and some of them are lost, insecure people. And yes, some use drugs, etc. But what about all those mixed up people who instead of traveling, they happen to be going to some college or other and then end up getting drunk at their fraternity house – what's the difference? There are unhappy people everywhere and I'll tell you, most of the people I've met have graduated from college and before getting a job they won't be able to get away from, they've decided to travel. Kathy and Jeff have NOT been on the road for the entire time. Two years ago they spent 10½ months traveling; five of those months in Greece, then on to Nepal. They wanted to see more, so after going home to Ohio to earn some money they returned to the East. Jeff has a degree in European history, and he's a registered carpenter. Kathy has her degree in English literature. Now they are headed to Australia, via Indonesia. Before they left the states they bought 65 acres of land in Arizona – quite something to go home to – but since that will be there no matter when they get there, their reasoning is why shouldn't they see and experience other parts of the world?! They'll probably work in Darwin as Jeff's carpentry should come in handy as all of Darwin must be rebuilt because of a big cyclone. And then they'll head back this way.

I love Nepal… I imagine that when I get home I'll be dreaming about returning to the Himalayas.

All I hear about in the little international news I do get are bad things happening in the US; recession with things getting harder every day… I do wish I already had an education behind me – an academic one, that is – because to tell you the truth – besides seeing everyone I've missed so much – the states don't sound like too pleasant a place to be right now. And though I do plan to go to college I can't say I'm looking forward to the academics; not my thing. I think it's unfair for you to pity and feel sorry for ALL the young people traveling. Sure, some are looking for themselves and instead remain frustrated and unhappy. But the majority of people I've met have had lots to offer: musicians, writers, people who are buying things to resell in the states or wherever… There are so many people into so many different and fascinating lifestyles! I'm learning so much. What better education would there be in this world other than seeing this world with my own eyes? I have no intention of staying on the road forever. I'll be home before October, but believe me, as soon as I finish studying and earn a degree in special education or something, I'll probably travel some more. Although the way things sound it probably won't be possible to save money and travel costs will have quadrupled like everything else. I wish to see Indonesia, Africa, Thailand, Burma; this world is just so vast and I've seen only a little of it!

I'm sorry this whole letter seems like a lecture, or at best, defensive, but your letter upset me. I don't like to hear stereotypical judgments and generalizations pinned onto such a large number of people who are all so vastly different from one another. Anyway, I love you and I'll write again soon from Goa.

Love, Karen

CHAPTER ELEVEN

ARE WE STILL IN INDIA?

GOA

(Journal) Tuesday, February 4 - 5:40 pm

Well – I'm finally sitting in our house near Colva Beach in Goa. Such a beautiful place! So plush and green with palm trees, banana trees, flowers of all sorts. And down by the ocean, just ten minutes from the house – it's like something out of National Geographic. There are dark-skinned Goans hauling in tremendous loads of fish (mackerel), the sun glinting off their flipping bodies.

We're sharing the house with Stuart (from Charlestown, MA), Frank from Georgia as well as Cathy and Steve also from Georgia. Six is too many for this place, so tomorrow Cathy and Steve will probably move next door.

The bus ride from Bombay really was a trip. It left from Dipty's, full of freaks, including lots of French junkies all headed for Calangute and Anjuna Beaches. We decided that we'd come here to Colva Beach where we heard it's mellower, and sure enough, it is.

Anyway, 40 freaks riding through Bombay in a Mercedes Bus with left hand steering. It was driven by a German guy and had adjustable padded seats, great music – beginning with "Magical Mystery Tour" which was quite appropriate! Then "Low Sparks of High Heeled Boys" by Traffic, which is one of my all time favorites! I'd forgotten how good the Beatles and Traffic could sound. The people were a trip. Lots of junkies shooting, coke being snorted – I held tightly to my bag.

It's so good to be here in the tropics! I already went swimming and the water felt like a bath with small waves. The local men wear only loin cloths, although this isn't really a nude beach. Having time to play, to swim, to write, to THINK!

Yay; today there were fourteen letters waiting for me in Paraji! I feel so loved and it's great to feel caught up with everyone! But I've now got tons of writing to do! Time for another swim!

(Journal) Wednesday, February 5

Today Stuart, David, and I walked into the town of Margao. I have my period, have had too much sun and am feeling cruddy – couldn't even go shopping. Instead I just sat in a little restaurant in Margao and wrote to Nanny. It's hard to feel close – our worlds are so far apart – yet when I look back we've been such good friends for a long time. It felt so good hearing from everyone!

Fourteen letters waiting for me; 2 or 3 from Mom, 1 from Dad – I love them so much; such beautiful people full of wisdom and I miss them. A letter from Jeri (I'll write her tomorrow) and one from Debbie – she really is mature; has her shit together. And Grammy wrote to me as well. I hope she isn't too lonely without Grandpa. And Shaari wrote; poor Newman having lost his mother. And Linda Krause wrote… I do wonder what our relationship will be like when I get home. I know Suzy and I will be close as her letters are in a sense a comfort as I know mine are to her as well.

Nick and Ceddy wrote, and Ellen and Vicki – can't believe we may be seeing them in Nepal and we may even trek together! Wonder where Roy's gone to? What a creep not to write!

We didn't get back from town 'til 5:00 or so then we went to the well to get water. I've never used a well. It's fun – the local ladies freak out if you use the bucket because they're dirt so there are big clay pots to use instead. David couldn't see and broke one of them inside the well. So we helped each other shower – it really is a pain in the neck trying to get clean without running water – and having five – ten Goans (mostly kids) watching. Goa is really nice – the people so mellow – and smiling – it's hard to believe we're still in India! What a difference having everyone here be Christian.

Tomorrow I'm going to the beach – no going into town or anything heavy like that. The next day I'll cash a check – the money sure does slip by – wrote Vicki today – she sounds close – hope she'll bring us some good ole cash.

Had a great dinner of boiled prawns with a large cabbage and tomato salad – tomorrow we're gonna cook a great meal as we bought fruit and veggies today: tomatoes, potatoes, oranges, lemons for lemonade we'll make tomorrow. Frank said a bread man comes by and honks his horn at around 8:00. I don't know my way around yet and I don't feel relaxed. Today my period bummed me out – 'twas very uncomfortable walking to town in the fairly intense heat. I felt so weak, not feeling too good now, stomach – very tired. Swimming tomorrow (yeah!)! Wish I could lose weight easily.

(Journal) Thursday, February 6 – 10:00 pm

Just finished a nice 4-page letter to Jeri – I really do miss her – probably won't even recognize each other when I go home. Home – freaks me out thinking about it – still don't know what I'll do when I get there – sure I'll go to school, but where? And what will I study?!

Anyway – today was nice – cooked up some eggs for breakfast – only 45 Np egg and then we headed toward the beach – walked a mile or so to a quieter beach – still lots of freaks around – there's no getting away from them! Tomorrow I'm gonna head in the other direction – in search for a bit of solitude. Tonight was nice – staying in for once – while everyone else went out – cooked up a good veggie curry for me, Dave, and Stuart – Frank, Cathy, and Steve ate out.

Today I saw Maureen and Michael – almost didn't recognize Maureen – she looked older – and her 4 1/2 or 5 yr. old daughter was also with her – "Maya." They've been here since December – are splitting shortly – day or two – and we'll probably see them in Nepal. It's really nice meeting up with people over and over again – friends on the road – saying goodbye to Kathy and Jeff was really difficult – can't believe they're not gonna "appear" on the beach tomorrow – but I know the next time we meet will be in the states – probably Arizona – maybe Boston – Frank, Cathy, and Steve are good friends – they're going to Ceylon – but we'll definitely be meeting them in Nepal – perhaps we'll trek together – and Vicki and Ellen.

Guess I'm going to Margao first thing in the morning – got to change a travelers' cheque, buy a new clay water jug to replace the one David broke in the well, coconut oil, a sheet – maybe some silver jewelry – I wouldn't mind having an anklet like the one Cathy bought today – I want to mail that roll of film home, like I promised so long ago – also, buy candles, kerosene, oranges, watermelon, maybe some spices – maybe some pictures for the walls, although there already are quite a few –

Seems strange living amongst Catholics and seeing pictures of Jesus instead of all the Hindu Gods we've become accustomed to. We're renting the house from Rosie DeCosta – her husband Albert is in Dubai, in Kuwait – for 6 mos. – she says money is pretty minimal – she has four children – 2 girls, 2 boys – a cat, which meows a lot, a big black goat, whose milk she gives to her 1 yr. old daughter every morning and evening. And pigs! It's a strange feeling to shit and have a pig or two eagerly awaiting to gobble it up – they really are funny looking!

Time to get some sleep – if the damn mosquitoes will stay away – a mosquito coil and about 15 sticks of incense better do the trick! Nighty nite!

Thursday, February 6 - 7:45 pm

Dear Jeri,

I received both of your letters – the one you mailed to Kathmandu and the one to Goa – thank you so much for writing – I love hearing from you, and you know what? When I got to Panjim, the first thing I did was go to the post office and there were 14 letters for me! From Mom, Dad, Debbie, Grammy, Shaari, Linda Krause who said she sees you on the bus every now and then, and that you really are growing up! Getting taller by the minute – anyway – out of those 14 letters, of course I read yours first, like I always do!

Right now, I am sitting on a chair in our little house, using the corner of the one table to lean on. The rest of the table is a mess – piled high with mandarin oranges, limes (tonight I made up a big pot of fresh lime juice – using about 25 limes – the small kind)! Potatoes, onions, cauliflower, carrots, tomatoes, scallions, spices, such as curry powder, black peppercorns – there's a big stone just outside, upon which I grind the pepper, etc. with another smaller stone.

Since there's no electricity in our house, I'm writing to you by candlelight – I don't mind not having electricity – candles are just fine – but I do wish there was running water! We have to use a well which is about a two minute walk from the house. Have you ever used one? I haven't, and it sure takes some getting used to! It's a big well, like all the pictures of wells you've seen, with a rope on a pulley. It's really clean water – the way to tell is if frogs are living in the well, and sure enough, I saw one today.

A lady sits near the well all day long to make sure that no one contaminates the water in any way. The first time I went to get water I tied the big metal bucket to the rope and was just about to lower it down to the water but the lady yelled at me, saying never to use that bucked because it's dirty – use only clay jugs – they're really big and clumsy – about a foot and a half in diameter. So I slipped the ring at the end of the rope around the neck of the jug and began to lower it. But it was dark and I couldn't see, so all of a sudden the pot hit the side of the well and broke. Needless to say, I really was embarrassed. Tomorrow I have to go into town (Margao – only 5 kilometers away) to buy a new jug.

Our house is made of wood and plaster, with a tin roof. The walls are whitewashed, which always makes a place look cheery, and there are four good-sized windows with wooden shutters, two chairs, a bench, this table (which is against a wall and has a large mirror on it) and a few shelves – the only necessary thing missing is running water – but I'm getting used to it. At our house in Pokhara there was running water right out front, but it only ran for two hours in the morning and another two hours late in the afternoon. I don't mind cooking using water from jugs – or washing clothes in buckets – I've been doing that for quite a while – it's just after spending a day on the beach it's nice to take a shower – there are SO MANY little things we all take for granted; it's not 'til they're not available that we can appreciate them. Anyway – behind the house is a little outhouse made of dried palm leaves woven together. There's a big hole with a place for each foot – I'm very used to squatting as all toilets from Greece on east are this style. They actually are more sanitary than the sit-down type at home – for public use, that is.

There's no sewage system here – all garbage is fed to the goats, cows, water buffaloes, or pigs that roam all around. And you know what? I hope this doesn't disgust you too much, but there are big fat pigs hanging around each toilet waiting to eat whatever people leave for them! At first I was really "grossed out" but they (the pigs) really do keep the place clean, and don't worry – I never ever eat pork – or any other meat – except fish. I haven't eaten any meat in 3 or 4 months! But I'm careful to balance my diet otherwise.

Here at Colva Beach, in Goa, there's plenty to eat! Every day I watch the natives pulling in huge nets filled with small silver mackerel, all flopping about looking like jewels with the sun shining on them – and prawns – which are like shrimp, sort of – they taste so good! Sitting on the beach with palm trees behind me, and dark-skinned (almost black!) natives hauling in their nets, singing and smiling – their white teeth gleaming – and women walking by with really big baskets filled with fish balanced on their heads and literally thousands of seagulls flying around and around crying – swooping down to get the fish which have fallen from (through) the nets. And the hand-made boats – really – it's just like a picture you'd see in a *National Geographic* magazine – it's just so gorgeous here!

Yesterday I went into town to buy vegetables, toilet paper, candles, etc. (missed the bus which runs every two hours or so), so I walked the 2 1/2 or 3 miles – boy was I hot! It's about 85-90 every day and the sky is always blue. On the beach it's comfortable, but on the road it's boiling hot… But today I spent on the beach; endless expanse of white sand – lined with tall graceful palm trees, swaying in the constant breeze – the crystal clear blue water hitting the beach with gentle waves, and it's so warm! Right now I'm really hot because I was in the sun all day – I'm beginning to get a tan – I plan to not spend too much time in the sun as I know too much isn't very good for the skin.

Goa really doesn't seem like India at all! First of all, most of India's people are Hindus, so I've gotten very used to seeing pictures of various Hindu Gods everywhere – like all those rice prints David had, remember? And the colored prints also! All over India there are Hindu temples – some of them are really large

– others consist of only a teeny stone structure with maybe a picture of a God, such as Shiva, the destroyer, and a few offerings, like flowers or some fruit – and usually there's incense burning. But Goa was a Portuguese province for a long time, and most of the Goans are Catholics! So there are churches all around, instead of temples.

We're renting our house from a woman named Rosie DeCosta (sure doesn't sound Indian! I laughed when she told me her name – I couldn't help it – it's just so American) who has four children and lives in the other half of the house. She speaks only a little English – my Hindi isn't helping very much here because the language of Goa is something entirely different – I forget what it's called but I can't make any sense out of it! Besides, as there have been many tourists here over the years, most people speak English really well. Anyway, Rosie is really nice. Her husband is away on a cargo ship for six months – he's been gone only two so far. He only gets to stay home for a month between journeys. Poor Rosie has to take care of the house, kids, and animals all herself! Speaking of animals – dogs, cats, goats – Rosie has a big black goat which provides milk for her year-old baby (Rosie's baby, that is). Tonight we cooked up a delicious stew – curried vegetables, and I gave all the scraps – potato peelings, carrot tops, etc., to the very appreciative goat! And this afternoon I shared a piece of bread and a banana with a little monkey who is tied to a tree outside a small restaurant. The bananas here are the best in the world.

They're only three inches long and sort of chubby – they cost one rupee (12 cents) for 8 or 9 and they're so sweet! A very popular drink around here (for the westerners, that is) is banana milkshakes – mmmmm good! Also, the native alcoholic beverage is Fenny, which is made from either coconuts or cashews. I don't particularly like it – it tastes too strong for me – like whiskey!

So Jeri – what's new with you? It sounds like you got some nice Chanukah gifts! I'm sorry you haven't received that shirt – but you know what? It's probably too small for you anyway! I wish I could send things home to everyone, but it's just too costly, and involves too much time – of course I plan to bring lots of things home with me – ask Mommy to please tell me what dimensions she wishes me to look for, for their bedroom rug. I left her letter telling me, in Kathmandu. Also – exactly what colors. I doubt if I'll be able to find anything as large as she'd like for only $500, including postage. Would she like a smaller one in those colors? Also – Persian rugs are the finest quality – they improve with age and wear – whereas all others aren't guaranteed to last very long. I'll do my best, tell her!

Well – I plan to stay in Goa for a month or 5 weeks. I'll probably go visit other beaches – I've heard there's a really beautiful fresh-water lake in the northwest part of Goa so I intend to go there. But this state is small, so it's easy to get around. I'll be returning to Colva for mail, so write again!

I love you and miss you!!!!!   Karen

(Journal) February 7 - 11:10 pm

Went to Margao this morning. Changed money – 7.85 RP. for $ – but state Bank of India's rate was only 7.69. We met Andrea – from Los Angeles – I really feel drawn to her somehow – she's also Jewish and 18 – graduated last February – left the states in May with her 18 yr. old boyfriend. They split up fairly recently and she's here in Goa living for free with a Goan family. Reading her letter from her mother makes me sad – looking at someone in about the same position I'm in except Dave and I are still together – her parents really wish she'd come home – wanting her to fly out of Bombay – $ is on the way via neighbors. It still hurts me, thinking of Mom and Dad – how good they've been to me – trying so hard – only to have me throw it all away – defy their every value – disobey actually – sometimes I really wish I had waited – studied first – not lived on my own for a while – I really must gain more independence – it's all up to me – it's just not good leaning on people – from Mom and Dad's home – under David's wing – security is a pleasant warming feeling.

My feelings really are mixed – I wish I could go to so many places and spend time: Indonesia, Sri Lanka, and hearing Cathy and Steve talk about the Kulu Valley, Manali… and the Greek islands are calling me as well. I'm really glad I already have a plane ticket home, because that's one decision already made – when to go home. I figure we'll be back in Kathmandu by the third or fourth week in March. We'll probably stay in Nepal for two months – maybe more, most likely leaving in June to head westward. Depending on our money situation maybe we'll fly to Greece? That's a brand new idea I just this minute thought of, because the Greek islands really are beckoning to me – ahhh the Mediterranean. Depending on time, money, and most of all, frame of mind… maybe I'll fly home from Greece. Or maybe I'll be really tired of the road – or maybe I'll be up for cruising around Europe some more visiting people we've met.

I really would like to see Switzerland, Amsterdam – oh all over Europe! There are just so many – too many – trips to get into – it's amazing! It's pretty difficult to project to the future – the near future especially, as right now I sit on what has turned out to be my priceless blue pad with the gas lamp lit. David's trying to sleep, over to my left. Frank is also, on the other side of the room, and Stuart is outside. He got really sunburnt. Cathy and Steve are next door. Their room is nice – clean, white and has electricity.

This morning Emma was playing Santana – record or tape I don't know which. And yesterday Dean Martin and Bing Crosby were singing Xmas carols! It feels strange living amongst Catholics after being around Hindus and Buddhists for so many months. The next 3 days – actually, the 9, 10, and 11 of February – there's a festival held all over Goa. There will be plays, carnivals, dancing and I hear something big's supposed to be happening in Panaji – we'll probably mosey on up – maybe there's more mail for me!

So – in Margao there's a really great bazaar, with such varieties of so many things! We didn't buy much – nothing exotic, except a large clay jug to replace the one David had broken – and tonight I broke one trying to help a little girl lift the heavy filled container out of the well – I pulled too quickly – so I gave her a rupee – and I learned that I shouldn't be saying "Namaste" but to say something like "Deo bari Curu???" I knew I'd forget how to say it the same day I learned it! Anyway – it means "God be with you." I really can't make heads or tails out of their language – I forget what it's even called.

Finally got back from town at 2:45 – hot, tired and a bit grumpy – and headed straight for the beach and walked to the right about 3/4 of a mile. Feels nice to be alone

Note to self: REMEMBER – MAIL ROLL OF FILM!

The beach really is pleasant – got to watch out for those jelly-fish – a guy told me that yesterday a girl stepped on one and had difficulty breathing for the next 4 hours or so.

And then home for a great surprise meal of boiled shrimps! 6 rupees for 3 kilos! I'll have to write home about that. Half we dipped in lime juice (or salt) and the rest were boiled in chili powder – just the right amount of spice seeped through the shells. And the coconut bread we bought in town today tasted so fine!

Tonight we caught the tail end of a film shown by "The Children of God." Quite a crowd; Goan-western mixture with at least 100-200 people. Strange movie – total symbolism – hope no Goans have bad dreams!

And then we, all 6 of us, went to a little milkshake shop – I had a coffee/chocolate delicious shake – And next door they have coconut chockies – fudge really – so chewy, sweet, succulent, obsessing – the best goody in Goa – I'm convinced!

Tomorrow I want to do some playing – perhaps I'll take my flute to the beach – although sand would probably mess it up. Maybe I should look for a bamboo flute – but they're not any fun compared to my beautiful silver Gemeinhardt. It's late – and I hate to spend 1/2 the morning lying in bed. Good night dear diary. Tomorrow I'll start putting some color into you! I'm so happy to have you in my life after having lost the other two (still totally bums me out to have lost not only my writing, but so many contacts of other freaks we met on the road).

(Journal) Saturday, February 8 - 2:10 pm

I sure am getting color now! My back is burnt to a crisp – really – and I'm sure by tonight I'll be hurting a lot more – I'm glad I don't burn ALL the time, it's just all this intense sun on usually unexposed parts of my body. But in a week or so I shall be black! Been putting coconut oil on it which just made me burn even worse…

Woke up early this morning and went to a little restaurant where I had a cold coffee (my latest obsession) and a fine onion omelet. Dave had a good sized piece of king; best fish I've had yet!

Then we headed to the beach and met up with Stuart. Did some exercises for a while – swimming's the best, then played Frisbee.

Two Goan guys came along and asked us if we'd like our ears cleaned. Sounded like a cool adventure. I can't believe all the crap – wax, coconut oil, sand – and in my right ear – a stone! He wanted one rupee for the cleaning – and asked for 10 rupees because of the stone – claimed some bullshit about medicine – showed me a bottle – think it was peroxide. Anyway – my ears feel cleaner than they ever have, and my guess is he put the stone in there just to be able to charge those 10 rupees! Makes for a great story…

(Journal) Sunday, February 9 - 10:00 pm

Now I'm sitting in Cathy and Steve's room – looking back on today. Got up early – awakened by the bread man's horn. We bought two big chapattis and I finished the picture on the previous page. We hung around – and finally went with Cathy and Steve to the crossroads just 10-15 minutes walk from here to see what was happening at the carnival. The only thing festive was a little kid, selling party hats. There were two freshly slaughtered pigs – how could anyone eat pork – my god – that's asking for hepatitis… It's quite a feeling to shit and have 2 or 3 big pigs wriggling in anticipation below… probably wondering "What does this next meal consist of?"

Anyway – Dave and Frank got back from town saying that everything except fruit stands was closed. They bought 74 oranges (small

ones) for 8 rupees and 12 bananas for a rupee! Headed to the beach at around 1:30 via our little milkshake shop. Oh yeah, I did some playing today and a little reading. I'm feeling so lazy – spaced. It could be the heat, but I think I'd better lay off the charas for awhile – budees also. I hope to feel more energy soon.

So we bought a whole basket of shrimps for only 10 rupees (hassled over the price) – and cooked them up. 1/2 we ate plain boiled and the rest we boiled with pepper and chiles which I had to grind with the mortar and pestle. I must say I do wish we had running water at least for showers as a well can be a pain in the ass!

Already, Dave's broken one clay jug and myself another as I was helping a little girl pull up her jug I pulled too fast. Stuart dropped a jug down and Dave climbed down to fish it out.

A little 7 yr. old child died today; she lived right below Emma's house (where Cathy and Steve are staying) and the funeral has lasted all day long right at the home. Then, at sunset, a procession with some dressed in white with small red capes – headed toward the church – singing softly. So eerie…

Again we headed to the crossroads to find some action. While we stood at the little store munching peanut butter on puffed rice chickies, an open-backed van cruised slowly down the street, with our four or five man band playing in the back.

As we walked toward the beach, we came across a crowd of people gathered around 3 musicians – drum, trumpet, and there were two guys dressed like women – falsies (which were uneven) and dangling earrings. The band moved on, but we decided that a milkshake took priority. Milkshakes finished (in other words, no milkshakes due to ice finished) at our place.

So we went to the Golden Sands that turned out to make lousy shakes. It was a frustrating evening – we just couldn't find a thirst-quenching drink – I'm so thirsty now…

The bar Vincy's really does jump in the evenings. There must have been at least 110 freaks in there – the crowd was a bit bewildering.. I don't like that place. The waiters are all schmucks.

So tired I keep dozing off – didn't sleep much at all last night – goddamn mosquitoes everywhere. But caladryl helps out a real lot…

(Journal) Monday, February 10

My new magic marker I bought in Panajin… have to get more. Dave got a letter from his mother and we heard from Jerry C. which was nice. Got back to Margao at around 4:00 pm to find people having a great time. All the guys throwing water and colored powders and dyes on all the women and girls. Dave and I both got it as we walked through the "Municipal Gardens." There's a circus in town! Decided not to go as we were too hot and sweaty and dirty –in need of a swim.

Had a good meal – king fisher and a large tomato, cabbage and beets salad – topped off with a banana shake. I really should fast – tomorrow I'll give it a try. Wish I liked the yogurt they serve around here.

Said good-bye to Jack and Paige – such beautiful people. I almost cried – gonna miss them – maybe won't see them 'til I make it to Seattle which is so far away. They're heading toward Ceylon on a bus leaving here tomorrow at 5:00 am to head to Madras. I admire Jack. That's quite a responsibility traveling with a child. I don't think I couldn't handle it – taking care of myself is enough for the time being.

Anyway – I'm exhausted – gotta sleep now after I brush my teeth – thinking maybe there might be another cavity on my lower right. Glad we'll be in Bombay in awhile so I can find a dentist.

Good, good night

(Journal) February 11

Another day has gone by, a week just slipped by – where did it go? Relaxing… it's just so easy to let the sun, sea, salt, and sand take me away with its timelessness. When it's hot I find it hard to motivate myself. I know I should be constantly exercising – getting my body in shape – as I still feel fat. It's such a curse – me and my sweet tooth – ain't fair! Milkshakes, chickies, cookies – goddamn I have no will power!

Went to the beach – and what else is new – bigger waves than usual – fun body-surfing – but my chest has peeled and burned again – it's stinging so much – don't know what's with me – for the first time in my life I'm not tanning – burnt only on my chest – the rest of me staying white, except my face is pretty dark.

Tomorrow Dave is heading up the beach – five hours or so to Betule. I don't feel like it tomorrow – have to premeditate such a big step – I guess Goan Paralysis is setting in. Actually, I'm bored – the heat is draining; makes me feel unmotivated. It's okay for a short while – so I'll probably join Cathy and Steve the next day and meet Dave there.

Must write to Dhana – and home. I guess I do write more letters than anyone else – I like writing – and I know how good it makes people feel to hear from me. Must write Grammy – wonder how she is since Grandpa died so recently…? And what she's decided to do about the house… and how's everyone else??? I really do miss everyone – February 14 – Valentine's day – can't believe it's been over 4 months on the road – how much longer? Definitely by Oct. 6 – going to utilize that plane ticket. I'd love to fly to Europe – but I want to see Bande Amir and Mazarishariff – oh, I don't know – glad I'm returning to Nepal – love it there – couldn't take weather any hotter than now – it would be stifling! As it is – I don't find it very pleasant to be in Margao or Panaji – too damn hot! Can't get into shopping or anything. Bitchiness sets in – hope I get mail soon – so tired and it's only 9:35 – is my watch right? Who knows… I like having my watch – it's impossible to escape from time – everyone's always asking me the time… yet they also tease me for wearing a watch. So tired – I've got to do something about this terrible sunburn on my chest – owww!!!!

(Journal) Wednesday, February 12

David just walked in – certainly wasn't expecting him, as this morning he left for Betul. I'd planned to join him along with Cathy, Steve, and Frank. My chest really is stinging – may even peel again – such a pain in the neck.

I didn't even go to the beach today; wrote to Grammy, and to Gail and mailed them along with Ellen's and Stuart's to his "old lady." Hope Ellen gets it – really hope Vicki gets the 7 pager we wrote…

Let's see – walking home from the Colva PO, saw a Goan lady sitting outside of her large house, making a pretty green and yellow plastic bag; damn strong and practical! I was thirsty and she looked lonely – bored. So I sat down. Three more ladies joined us, so interested in what's happening in our western world... They can't understand all the freaks (neither can I) walking around half nude. They wanted me to explain meditation and asked me how I dress at home in the states. One of the Goan ladies was tiny and wearing a pink and white dress reminding me of Lucy.

Heard from Grammy and Daddy today – both were beautiful letters. A new car! Seems there's a letter I haven't received from Mom – they are a together bunch of people.

I must begin to make some decisions. I know I want to go to school and in some ways I think I should go to a regular old academic college after all. I'm going to be living there... don't know about Friend's World – sounds great, but not 'til I know what I want exactly want to study. Need to think it through...

Ate a good meal at the vegetarian restaurant in Margao – though nothing's been as good as Dhana's cooking. Must drop her a line...

February 12

Dear Grammy,

And another beautiful day has dawned here at Colva Beach in Goa. It's now 8:30 AM, sunny yet still cool. I'm sitting outside our house, watching everyone going about their daily business. Cathy, who lives next door, is returning from the well with a brass jug balanced on her hip and a bucket in her other hand; Frank (from North Carolina) is reading Armageddon, by Leon Uris; Stuart (Boston) is flossing his teeth; two of the little Goan children are playing with our frisbee which I'm so glad we thought to bring!

There are chickens roaming about, and dogs, and goats, and big fat pigs waiting by the outside palm frond toilets for their next meal – yuck! Don't worry – I don't eat meat – only fish. And I've been eating very healthy lately, cooking every other day or so. Shrimp cost 2 rupees a kilogram, and veggies are reasonable but require a trip into Margao to purchase.

I don't like going into town as it's just so hot once I'm away form the beach. But here it's pleasant and breezy – though it's impossible to be on the beach between 12:00 and 2:00. The intense midday sun should not be under-estimated!

I've just been rereading some of the letters I've received – 14 in Panjim and 6 in Bombay. Daddy's letters are great – actually every single letter is great! I'm glad Debbie found a chessboard for the set I sent!

The last three days have been crazy. Because Goa was originally a Portuguese province, most Goans are Catholic, so pre-Lent festivities have been happening. There's a circus in Margao, and all over the place men and boys run about wearing masks and carrying squirt guns and containers of white and blue powder, which they throw all over the women and girls – and they just love to get the westerners – Dave and I got it really good when we were in town the other day – thank heavens the blue washes out! David left early this morning – heading down the beach to a little town 5 hours away. I may head down that way tomorrow or the next day – today I'm nursing a little sunburn – for some reason my chest has peeled and then reburned – oww! I'm not tanning as quickly as usual – though of course David is black; he practically looks like a native. He's lost about 15 lb. and he's exercising and gaining weight now. Seems like most men lose weight while traveling in this part of the world – whereas women gain – and I'm no exception! It's just not fair that I should gain so easily – and I would have a sweet tooth… guess it runs in the family. There are milk shake stands along the beach – and delicious assortments of sweets such as little round peanut clusters that taste like cracker jacks kind of – called "chickies" and only cost 10 paisa each. Anyway – I'm on a diet. Instead of milk shakes I'm drinking limes and soda water and for dinner I'm eating fish and a cabbage and tomato salad. At restaurants a nice big piece of king fish is served with salad, costing only 2.50 Rps (30 cents!) So we're living very cheaply here but still our money is dwindling… Friends of ours from Watertown, Vicki and Ellen, are heading this way shortly. We've asked them to bring us some cash – American dollars are in much demand here. For some reason it's illegal for Indians to purchase dollars, yet in order for an Indian to leave the country, he must show foreign currency – they're just asking for corruption!

So Grammy – I really haven't much else to say as all I've been doing lately is writing in my new diary which is a nice big hard-cover red book with no lock and key like my other one. Write to me cuz I love hearing from you. I hope my last letter wasn't offensive. I was just a little indignant that you were generalizing so. I hope all is well at home and stay skinny! I hear you're looking good!

Love you!
Karen

(Journal) Thursday, February 13

Chest still burning – woke up early today – instead of walking all the way to Betul – we took the bus to Margao – and then on to Betul. Buses take so long… it was a rough walk with

my sun-burn – such a curse! Had to climb – really sharp rocks which were difficult with thongs.

Finally made it to a cliff overlooking a rocky beach with large waves hitting the shore with a crash… We climbed down the cliff, amid so many palm trees – all full of ripe coconuts. Dave and Frank and Steve tried climbing the trees as there were steps cut all the way up – except for the last 10 ft. or so deliberately to prevent people like us from stealing their coconuts.

After awhile a couple of Goans cut 11 coconuts down for us and charged us 3 for a rupee, plus 6 mugs. We got them all open with Goan machetes. Such sweet milk – unlike the fermented stuff people have tried to sell me at Colva.

And now it's dark – can hardly see to write. It's so peaceful – waiting for supper at the home of some nice Goans. We saw a Goan fisherman who was so friendly. He had feet like Nepali feet (makes me think of hobbit feet!). He says he's been to Boston, Russia, Germany, etc. I guess with the navy…

Anyway – we asked him where we could eat. He brought us here. Turns out that the English guy and his French girlfriend

Had to come back before sunset to put some oil on my chest – can't believe how goddamn painful it is. Perhaps I'll spend the day here tomorrow. Really can't stand the sun at the moment – don't understand why my skin's goofing up so much – I should be black by now. David blends right in of course and looks so beautiful. His body's really getting strong and in shape.

We made a shade structure to protect us from the midday sun.

who used to live next door to us at Colva are staying here.

On a plateau high above the ocean there's an old fort crumbling. Inside there's a quaint little white church.

I walked almost to the far side from where I could see the ocean on both sides. There were mountains off in the distance and tremendous rocks jutting out all over. It's all is so green – palm trees are everywhere.

(Journal) Valentine's Day, February 14

Decided not to stick around – had to pay 5 rps each for a rice meal which wasn't too great – coconut and fish curry – strange combo. Plus, after all the coconuts we'd eaten yesterday, don't think I'll be eating any for a long time.

We were gonna go to a Catholic mass to watch little kids having their first communions. All dressed in white, they and the priest marched in a procession – trumpet and drums playing – really nice.

Walked and walked – so hot – goddamn chest bothers me more than ever – maybe tomorrow it'll feel better.

Hi all,

As I think I've mentioned before – most Goans are staunch Catholics. We were awakened yesterday morning by drum beats and a trumpet. Marching by the house, toward the church, was the priest wearing white robes with a red shoulder cape and carrying a silver staff accompanied by about ten people, with 3 or 4 others also wearing red and white. We followed them down the road and through the crumbling ruins of a tremendous fort I hear was used by the Portuguese against the Indians. And then on to the church – a small white structure – lots of little boys and girls dressed in white for their first communions – it's hard to believe this is part of India – really! So different! A relief from the intensely crowded cities filled with so much human misery.

So – we began walking at around 8:30 AM – 10 kilometers walk ahead of us through lush forests – up a small mountain – 6-7 hundred ft. – finally we made it to the village of Agunda where we could catch a bus back to Margao.

I've decided that I don't really like the tropics as I'm not simply not comfortable here; too damn hot! I'm still getting over the worst sunburn I've ever had – my chest peeled and burnt again to a crisp – it's at the flaky, itchy, stinging stage now. There's lots of biting insects around (I'm taking malaria pills every Monday). I'm really looking forward to returning to Nepal,

which will be very shortly! Probably leave Goa by March 1 – spend 3-5 days in Bombay – go to Delhi long enough to get new Nepali visas – and then to Nepal. Hope to be there by the 3rd week in March. Letters from all of you take 8 days to reach me so if you wrote to New Delhi SOON I'd probably receive it – but after March 1, please just write to Am. Exp. Kathmandu! Dad – please send me an absentee ballot if possible. When's the election anyway? You could mail it to Am. Exp. Bombay if you think it can be there by March 4 or 5.

I love you all – this letter's not one of my best – sorry – I'll write again soon.

Karen

(Journal) Tuesday, February 18

Haven't written even in my journal because I haven't done anything except lie in bed. Woke up Saturday morning with good ole egg burps – figured I had dysentery so didn't eat. So weak – Saturday and Sunday. Read *1984* for the 2nd time. So little motivation to do anything – let my clothes soak for 3 days as I didn't have the energy to rinse them out. Turns out I may have hepatitis which is a royal bummer. Can't really say I'm surprised – no one ever called Nepal a clean country! And I was there six weeks ago and I hear hep has a six week incubation period from the time of exposure. So day after tomorrow I'll head for Bombay – it's so good I got sick here – because Dhana will take care of me – damn – I don't want to go home yet – I must get back to Nepal – haven't seen enough of it! Just wrote to the farm and to Mary Sarclay – wonder how they're all doing – wonder where Roy is and if we'll really meet up with Vicki and Ellen??!!! I really am looking forward to seeing them. And I'm determined to go back to Nepal!!!!

It's really too bad I haven't been able to really enjoy Goa – what with my chest being burned and now getting sick – my luck really hasn't been to good lately – that's for sure! Also – Dave's foot being paralyzed has me a bit scared – right now he's seeing a doctor in Margao – hope something comes of it.

Well – transition time – tomorrow I'm flying to Bombay – yes, that's right – flying and only 1/2 an hour – hope Dhana's at home – will call her from the airport – mixed feelings now – leaving here isn't so hard – can't be in the sun – the heat drains me – so what good is it being in Goa? Leaving David for a short time – good for us both – collect our thoughts – it's not easy spending 24 hours a day with anyone!

And tonight I met Ulla – feeling so close – yet having to go our various ways – I know we'll meet again in Nepal – must leave note for her at Poste Restante…

Wish I'd met Ulla sooner – felt oh-so-close to her – hopefully we'll meet again in Kathmandu – that last night at Vincy's was nice – good people – sat for awhile with Jenny, Peter, and what's his name – they're all from the same town in Eng. – they live in the same house as Andrea – met them that day I was feeling so lousy and Andrea took me home – wonder how she's doing – so lost – I do sympathize! Poor kid – what a schmuck her boyfriend turned out to be.

Said good-bye to Ian and Bruce – who brought my wonderful hair brush to me – from when I left it in that crazy hotel room in Gorakhpur the night before I got ripped off – oh God – what a nightmare – let's see – there were 7 of us – Sharon and Martin – must keep in touch – Bruce and Ian and Marty – hope the picture Dave took comes out – all of us lined up trying to sleep.

(Journal) Thursday, February 20

Poor Baba at Vincy's – short – maybe 5'6", very dark – must be at least 50 – dancing around to the music – wanting baksheesh – took him out for baju at the crossroads the other day – Looking back now – at my short stay at Colva Beach –

Unfortunately I can't say I thoroughly enjoyed myself – for the first few days I did, but then that burn on my chest was oh-so uncomfortable – walking to Agunda was pretty horrible – I mean – the scenery was gorgeous – the real tropics – so lush and green… but I felt so miserable – pain from that sunburn had me in tears!

I know I'm too pessimistic – and I complain too much, but damn… it seems like rotten things keep happening to me – the sun burns, being ripped off and now being laid up with hepatitis – it's really a goddamn drag!!! I'm really wanting to head homeward.

"Homeward Bound, I wish I were…"

Yet I'm scared of reaching there – don't know what to expect after the initial hugs and kisses – I must be strong – hold my head up – because if I'm feeling lonely now, I think my loneliness will be much greater – because I will be faced with myself – and only myself – and having to make REAL decisions – yes – Karen, your reality stems from 67 Bright Rd. in Belmont, Mass. – you've got to face it – and the sooner you do, the better for you – look from within – you've shit upon yourself for years now – literally – you owe it to yourself to become someone – someone who is strong and respected by others – love isn't enough when respect is lacking.

And in Agunda – or whatever the name of that village with the old crumbling fort – where we stayed in the same house that English John and Claudine – his French girlfriend who was sick – lived in – and they used to live next door to us at Colva; such nice people. Again – wish I'd gotten to know them better.

I wish I could jump back in time – re-live a lot of things differently, but since it can't be done – I'll have to use the wisdom I've gained through my travels – and over the years – to begin a new life as an individual; a grown up!

Thursday, February 20 - 2:30 pm

Hello!

Sorry I haven't written in a while (3, maybe 4 days?). The last letter I mailed was to Marilyn Barron – hope she received it (and let you all know). Anyway – at the moment I'm sitting in the Indian Airlines Office in Panjim, having just booked myself a ticket to Bombay on tomorrow's 2:30 PM flight. Somehow, the tropics and I don't seem to get along. I find it uncomfortably hot and it's even too warm at night for me to sleep easily. There are tons of insects always buzzing around and crawling all over me.

During the day I have felt totally unmotivated – drained of my energy – not wanting to do anything. I'd sure hate to be here in the summer! So, I'm returning to Bombay – where I know I'll be most welcome, once again, by Dhana. David will be staying in Goa for another week or two – then he'll join me in Bombay, and we'll head directly to Nepal. I can't wait to get back there! I'm even considering flying from Delhi to Kathmandu to avoid a few LOUSY train rides and a lot of time spent in going overland.

But flying is expensive… and my money is running really low. We've written to Vicki Boyajian, who's planning to head east and meet us in Nepal – and asked her to bring us $350 in cash. There's much better rate of exchange for dollars rather than cheques. In India it is illegal for Indians to purchase dollars, yet in order for an Indian to leave the country, he must show foreign currency! If that isn't asking for corruption, then I don't know what is. So – as you can imagine, there's quite a black market for dollars. Just now, when I bought my plane ticket in order for me to get the 25% youth fare reduction – I had to pay in either dollars (or travelers' cheques) rather than in rupees. The guy said it was the law – but I'll bet he just wanted the cash which wouldn't surprise me at all as the corruption goes RIGHT to the top in this mixed up country.

I really do have mixed feelings about India. I find it fascinating as there's so much to see and experience. I don't at all regret having come – yet I find myself hating it here, as well. There's just so much bureaucratic nonsense to put up with – as many people have said, "The Indians try to do things the way the British do – but they lack the mentality!" and I'll tell you – the majority – 99.9% – of Indians I've come across seem so damn stupid – though it's probably just my judgment based on such different cultural beliefs and customs. (Dad, you'd go crazy with the inefficiency compared to what we are accustomed to in the West!!)

I'm referring to those who hold jobs, such as booking airplane tickets. For example, for my date of birth the dumbass wrote June 13, 1972, which is when my passport was issued and bank clerks, or railway officials, or police – they've got to be the worst. Also, Indians like to stare – totally unabashed like little kids which in the West is considered rude. – i.e. when I'll enter a small restaurant and order a tea – every person will stop what they're doing and with their ugly bug-eyes, stare at me – crowds even gather on the street – Yuck!

As I said, I can't wait to get to Nepal. There the people all smile and say "Namaste" with their hands brought together at their foreheads. Yes, I admit there are good places in India – Benares was amazing – and Bombay is so exciting. I'm planning to do some buying for myself and others in Bombay – everything the world has to offer (materialistically speaking) is available there!

There's a silver bazaar and street after street lined with little silver shops – so far on my trip I haven't bought anything for myself or for anyone else – I've always told myself to wait – that I may come across something I like better – now of course I'm kicking myself for not having bought so many beautiful things…

In Bombay I'll look for a rug for Mom – PLEASE send me the measurements again – I left them written on a pad with the stuff I stored in Nepal accidentally. So far in Margao, I've received a letter from Dad, Grammy, Mom (with the pretty piece of material enclosed), and two from Sue Jablow. She and I have been writing to one another quite a bit – more than anyone else. I consider her to be a good friend, and I know she'll be there when I get home. Also – Gail and Nancy and Linda K have written – it feels so good to hear from people – to know that they care.

I must admit to being homesick – but I can't leave the East until I've returned to Nepal which I can't get enough of it! When I come home I intend to begin studying right away – special education. I realize how difficult it will be for me to go back to school after this long break, Mom's suggestion that I should maybe begin by going to night school, "to get the hang of it," is a good one.

Sorry this letter is so disjointed and sounds negative… I'll write from Bombay tomorrow or the next day. Please write to me c/o Dhana Goradia, 153 S.V. Road, Vile Parle, Bombay, India, until I let you know you otherwise.

Love you all,
Karen

(Journal) February 21

This has been quite a day – said good-byes last night to Bruce and Ian – good guys, gonna miss'em – perhaps I'll see them at home in '76. Anyway – also said bye to Liz, the Aussie we met first at the good ole Earth Restaurant in Kathmandu. Her husband Tony and she are nice; wish I'd spent more time with her. It's a strange feeling to feel so close to new friends and have to say goodbye with no idea if I'll ever see them again.

Left the house at 8:30 AM and caught a taxi at the crossroads after one last tea. Banks weren't open yet – neither was the "Shaliman", the really nice and cool restaurant with the low tables and really comfortable chairs. They serve amazing Russian salads – mmmm – have good music and a great atmosphere. I wish we'd discovered it sooner.

No mail today – but yesterday when I went to Panjim (to book my flight) there was a letter from Gail, Dad, Mom, a beautiful letter from Cedric – picture of him enclosed – and a letter from Kathy and Jeff from Thailand – yay! It was great hearing from them – poor Roy! Both Cedric and Kathy told us he was charged by a Yak up by Periche and his knee gave out – bad – he's probably home by now!

Anyway – took the airlines van from the Margao Office – left at 12:00 – saying "bye for now" to Dave was strange – it broke us both up a little, but it's for the best – a chance for me get my head together and to take the time I need to get well.

Got to the airport at around 1:00 and waited til 3:00 for take-off. We spoke with a woman from New Zealand who's been working in their embassy in Delhi for 3 1/2 yr. and was heading back to NZ – is a bit scared as that's a long time to have been away! And a really nice couple from Ohio – so all-American – she looked like Miss Curry. I always feel drawn to straight tourists – older ones.

The flight was nice. I asked for a window seat and got one, even though it was over the wing I could still see beautiful Goa with its ubiquitous palm trees. I watched as we flew north, getting further and further away and miniature boats sitting upon the glistening waters of the

Arabian Sea – and the western coast of India. We followed it right up to Bombay. We were served biscuits (I got 4 Ritz crackers in a little cellophane Indian Airlines packet) and fruit juice.

It was only a 45 minute flight. At the airport I went to the tourist center at the Bombay airport and had them phone Dhana for me. To my TOTAL DISMAY, I learned that she left yesterday, with her sister Hemlata to visit another sister in Gujarat – she won't be home for 10-15 days! I really freaked – but the grandma told the guy I should come anyway…

So here I am. Dhana's oldest sister is staying here while Dhana's away. She also speaks NO English. Mukesh came and took me to see Dr. Desai – same doctor Dave went to for his foot – the dentist's father. I kept crying – just a little – admit that I'm feeling so alone – totally helpless – lonely – vulnerable, scared – went to Teju's mother's house. Sat around waiting 'til I had to piss – so I could give a sample for the Doc – it came out coke-colored. He took one look and said "yes" and told me to take good ole Liv 52's and another pill – and to drink 2 glasses of sugar cane juice per day – so we bought a bottle which sits in the fridge – and he instructed me to eat only fruit and rice and dal. I only pray that I'll get well quickly – must rest for 4 days – not going out at all – I'll be a great patient!

Little Roopa remembers me – name and all. She was in such a good mood tonight – we'll have a good time together – time to sleep.

CHAPTER TWELVE

INDIAN HOSPITALITY IS THE BEST!

BOMBAY

SIDE NOTE – APRIL, 2018

While in Goa, we took a long hike during which I became weak, necessitating a bus ride back to our village in lieu of hiking back with our friends. The local medicine man looked at my eyes, my palms, and nail beds, then poked me in the lower gut and announced that I had "the jaundice" (aka hepatitis A). So I went to the local hospital to have a blood test. There I waited in line for a couple of long hours along with hundreds of locals who looked far sicker than I did. By the time I got to the front of the line and asked for my blood to be drawn in order to tell if I did indeed have hepatitis, I was told it would take two weeks for them to get test results.

Subsequently I decided it would be best for me to simply fly back to Bombay where I knew I'd be well cared for by the family in Bombay. Meanwhile, I knew that if Dad heard I was sick he'd probably be on the next plane to Bombay in order to rescue me. Determined to continue my travels it was paramount for me to NOT let my family know I was sick! This would require me to ask the Indian family to please not tell their family in Boston, to which they graciously agreed.

Saturday, February 22

Hello!

Again I write home from Bombay, from the home of Dr. Shah's mother, sister and two-year-old daughter. Yesterday I said good-bye to David in Margao, and took an Indian Airlines shuttle bus to "Debdim," the only airport in Goa. My flight wasn't due to leave until 2:30, and I arrived there before 1:00, which gave me plenty of time to talk with some of the other travelers. There was a woman from New Zealand who's now heading home after spending the last 3 1/2 yr. working for her embassy in New Delhi. And a super nice couple from Ohio; he's a technical engineer for Madras Rubber Industries and this is his 4th or 5th trip to India with all expenses paid for him and his wife. And of course there were lots of Indians traveling home to Bombay.

Most Indians especially in the south speak English, even to one another and they just love speaking with tourists: "From which country are you coming from?" Their strange British-Hindi accents are difficult to understand, they always use too many words and they tend to speak so fast! I say I'm from Boston, and I'm usually met with a blank look, so I add, "Near New York" – then the dawn of recognition – "Oh yes, I know New York, I have a sister living in Los Angeles." It really is funny sometimes.

A guy on the airport shuttle said, "I hear that in America students bring guns to school and shoot each other, and that they put their feet up on their desks. These things don't occur in Indian schools…" There are ignorant people in the world. He was speaking with total sincerity! And I know this was said in response to the international media coverage of the riots happening in response to desegregation in American schools.

I asked for a window seat and got one, but it was over the left wing. Luckily I could still see the sparkling Arabian Sea below and beautiful palm tree-lined coast of Goa. The palm trees continued throughout the entire 45-minute flight all the way up the coast to Bombay! As we followed India's western coast and further from Goa, things began to get brown with interesting land including plateaus jutting up and square plots of farmland. I'm told that even flat land here must be terraced to prevent the monsoon rains from washing away the topsoil.

It was a small plane and we were served fruit punch and a little cellophane Indian Airlines packet of Ritz-like crackers by the one flight attendant. The next thing I knew we were on our way down to the bustling metropolis of Bombay – the New York of the East you might say.

I had the tourist agency at the airport call Dhana's for me. To my great dismay Dhana (she's the one who speaks English as she lived in the states) is away visiting a sister in Gujarat State and won't be back for two weeks. But her mother said I should definitely come anyway, the only problem would be language. So I came to find another of Dhana's sisters staying with her mother, neither of whom speak any English whatsoever. They don't even speak Hindi! Their native language is Gujarati. Let me explain. Dr. Shah (he) is the youngest of 7 children, and I think the only guy, and his six sisters live in Bombay. So after a very frustrating hour or so during which we were not able to communicate, little Roopa appeared with a cousin Mukesh. He's 20 years old and is a science major at a local college. He speaks English very well! It turns out he's also staying here while his aunt Dhana is away caring for Roopa. Yay! I lucked out.

So, once again I've been made comfortable and invited to feel right at home. I've returned to Bombay for a number of reasons. First, I just wasn't feeling up to par in the south – it was too damn hot! Bad sun-burn caused me not to feel well – as I explained in my letter written and mailed Thursday the 20th. I was feeling unmotivated and drained.

Second, I felt I needed to be alone – that is away from David for a bit. We're getting along fine, but I do need a chance to think about me uninterruptedly. In Goa there were just too many distractions with other westerners all around. Many interesting people. But you know me – I have a habit of letting myself be distracted to avoid thoughts and feelings – a very bad habit which I'm trying to change.

I do wish I already had a college education behind me – or at least part of one. I'm definitely planning to go to school AS SOON AS I return. Mom's idea of night school to help me get back into studying is a good one. I'm still very keen on working with retarded children – visiting that school for the retarded here in Bombay confirmed this thought. Dave will pick up any other mail that is sent there for me – and just after I mailed my last letter home on Thursday, I received a letter from Dad. He wrote it back on January 6!

Love, Karen

(Journal) Sunday, February 23

Well – today has finally come to an end… damn, there are just so many hours, minutes, and seconds. My diet today consisted of: one cup of tea this morning, a glass of delicious cold and refreshing sugarcane juice, and a glass of barley water which is a bit sweet and not at all bad tasting. All I could think of was Mary Poppins – when Jane and Michael Banks sang their song seeking a nanny – only time I've ever even heard of barley water! Anyway, it makes one urinate really often; in and out of the bathroom all day. But I'm happy to report that my pee looks normal-colored today after looking like coca cola for the past week. However, there's a new development – mucous in my shit – yuck – actually scary.

For lunch I was served a bowl of plain boiled (cold) rice and a glass of buttermilk yogurt with all the fats taken out, tolerable mixture with salt added but by no means delectable… I ate a mandarin orange or two, drank another glass of sugarcane juice, the rest of the barley water (glass and a 1/2) and a whole lot of roasted chickpeas, which really are good. This was followed by yet another cup of tea. Then for dinner a rice and dal mixture, only slightly flavored, but good. I really am lucky – these people are just so amazingly hospitable! If it weren't for them I'd probably be home by now or at least as far west as Europe.

Felt so depressed today, really wanting to go home. I read over all the letters I've received since Bombay three weeks ago; quite a number. It feels so wonderful to KNOW people care. I really do have a beautiful family – couldn't ask for more! I love them all so much and just want to go home!

Also must return to Nepal … it's difficult to say at this point. It depends on my health. Nepal just isn't the place to be if my system is very weak. I may not be able to trek. Speculating is being unfair to myself – just need to wait and see how things go over the next few weeks.

Tonight Mukesh, Roopa and I went for a walk. The weather is really pleasant and I am grateful to have broken the monotony of convalescence a bit, anyway!! Until tomorrow…

Tuesday, February 25

Hello!

I write to you now from Bombay – where I am staying at the home (apt.) of the family of some Indian patients of my Dad's. It feels great to be welcomed, to be able to put down my bags, sit back with my feet up, and get waited on… Indian hospitality amazes me – it's all I've heard plus so much more. The family is such a tight unit: cousins, aunts, brothers, sisters always visiting one another. I feel like a VIP as they all want for me to join them in their respective homes for dinner. Such wonderful dinners are prepared! These people are Gujarati, which is one of the 22 main cultures and languages of India, originally from Gujarat State. Unfortunately, my small knowledge of Hindi is of no help whatsoever in speaking Gujarati – but luckily English is spoken by enough people for me to make my needs known. Anyway, like all Indian cooking, Gujarati cooking is highly spiced, though not overridden with chilies, which always make my eyes water and causes me to choke. It's more of a sweet spicy taste. These people are strict vegetarians who don't even eat eggs. At every meal a huge portion of rice is served along with a few (2, 3, or 4, depending) little dishes containing various veggie curries, and dal soup (dal is the word for lentils, which are the main source of protein in the Indian diet).

I've come to really enjoy Indian food and am gonna miss it! And of course chapattis are served. They're wheat flour and water dough which is rolled into pancakes and cooked in a flat pan. It's best to put them right into an open fire so they puff up and become a bit crunchy. If it's not chapattis, then puris take their place, which are smaller, also made from wheat flour, but rolled out and then deep-fried which gives them a flying saucer-like appearance. You see, Indians (of ALL classes) don't bother using silverware. Instead they just break off pieces of chapattis or puris and use them to pick up their food. I've grown very accustomed to this habit and love it! My folks will probably find me totally uncivilized when I return home! And of course, as soon as I've taken a bite or two, a whole new serving (of everything) is heaped upon my plate and then again after that. It hurts their feelings for me to say no before I've had at least 3 helpings of everything!

Bombay is bustling; it's exciting, noisy, modern, ancient, ageless, diverse… Like all of India the best word to use is EXTREME! Double-decker buses, bicycles, cows roaming at will causing traffic jams, horse-drawn carts serving as taxis plus hundreds of small black and yellow taxis scurrying around. And Sikhs looking so regal in their gaily-colored turbans whiz by on motorcycles. Of course everyone drives on the left side of the road. So much of England's influence is apparent especially here in the south. Many people speak English; it's funny to hear Indians conversing with one another in English with their British-Hindi accents. I find them a bit difficult to understand at times as they speak so quickly! And there are even women in mini-skirts, although the majority wear saris. One of these days I'm going to buy myself a sari as I think they're really beautiful and so practical for this weather. It's unbelievably hot here – and so humid! If this is the end of the winter I sure would hate to be here in the summer when the monsoons happen.

Never will I be able to live in a place that doesn't have definite seasons – being here makes me appreciate New England. It's just SO different here from everything at home. There, in western society, one doesn't see much life in the streets. I'm not only referring to actual dwellings on sidewalks, but believe me here there are people, people everywhere living under the most deplorable conditions such as inside drain pipes! And under small dirty pieces of metal and cloth held together by faith… I'm talking about the fact that people sell everything imaginable for their existence: peanuts, haircuts, shaves, head massages, fortune telling, sugar cane juice (mmm!), oranges, guavas, bananas (best in the world!), lottery tickets, birds that sit on your shoulder chirping never to fly away, toys, underwear, pots and pans, pens and pencils, sweets of all sorts, ice cream, cigarettes, knife sharpeners walk around with tremendous sharpening stones, new and used paperbacks in every language you can name… And of course there are beautiful handicrafts for sale but I find it frustrating because everything that's available in shops here, I've seen in Indian shops in and around Boston though of course there's a big price difference... I admit I'm bored with it all at this point and am hoping to find something new!

So I hope you've been sharing letters and following me in my journeys...
Love,
Karen

(Journal) Wednesday, February 26

Again I visited Dr. Desai with a urine sample. Today it seems to be almost normal-colored, though later in the day it was again orange. Dr. says I'm 90% better, that instead of 6 Liv-52's per day, I should take only 3 and only 2 white tablets. I'm to continue on more or less the same diet, although I can have more variety, providing I eat nothing that's fried. He said I can have sweets – yay! All this shall be continued through March 10th which is when he thinks I should be fully recovered. I hope I don't have to stick around 'til then – and that Dave comes really soon – I'm going crazy with boredom!

And now I'm sitting outside the apartment building along with Roopa and Teju's mother, another two women and their two little boys. It seems to me that Indian women – at least these women that is – lead rather boring lives. Yesterday Mukesh's mother was sitting in the living room embroidering a sari. It was plain white khadi – red thread with a pattern printed out for her. She says she must do something other than read: "I can't read all the time – and I have nothing to do – I must cook" (she has four sons, Mukesh being her youngest). "Also, I must wash clothes." She has a teaching education, but she says she doesn't have time for all her work at home plus teaching what with all the corrections, etc. Jobs are very difficult to come by – such an understatement...

Perhaps I will see Hemlatta this evening and I will again visit her school. That would be nice... break up the boredom. Tomorrow won't be so dull after all. Teju's mother's neighbor teaches at a college run under the Ghandian philosophy and has invited me to accompany her...

– laughing, dancing, flashing white teeth in dark beauty faces – and long braids tied up – slender legs and bare feet – sparkling eyes – oh so pure – like a Himalayan stream tumbling down – playing, teasing – joyous laughter reverberating against the four walls of the small room – little girls everywhere are so beautiful – uninhibited – enjoying while it's still possible – doesn't matter what language – or walk of life – for the love of laughter – so joyous – is universal...

I love children so – they make me light up from within. And I know they feel connected with me as well. Little Roopa and I feel like we've become sisters though we speak different languages. It's okay, we manage to communicate somehow. And tonight – playing with another little 5-year-old beauty named Padmaja. She's so eager to learn! I sang "Where is Thumbkin" and both girls were totally entranced. Again – the language poses only slight hassles.

Yes. I will devote myself to working with children. I need them, and there are so many little ones who need me. This love will help me endure studying – it will give me the willpower I so desperately need.

I'm feeling better about me already – having the knowledge confirmed that I will go to school to become a teacher feels clear. I am smiling from within now… feeling good – strong!

"The love and wisdom of God are manifest not only in the gifted ones; but even in these broken fragments of humanity, which should therefore be carefully gathered up so that nothing be lost which His sanctifying fingers have touched."
—*Educating the Mentally Handicapped*
By Jai H. Vakeel

…Above all it is important that the parent and teacher should appreciate every little effort and applaud the smallest achievement so that the child finds a cheerful hope and a new meaning in every day of his life…

(Journal) Thursday, February 27

I walked to Varsha's apartment which is located just below Teju's mother's. Together we walked back to S.V. Road and caught a bus to Juhu, where her college is; a small school with only 90 students. First I was introduced to some of the teachers (all women) and to the "director" – a very jolly obese woman who used to be the principal at Hemlatta's school. Then I met the art teacher who showed me some incredible things done by students including woven shoulder bags, wall-hangings and amazing batiks. However, although the students did the waxing, all the designs were done by the teacher – and a local laundry does the actual dyeing! It disappoints me that an institute of higher education – especially one run under the Ghandian philosophy of self-sufficiency – doesn't encourage students to be original. Oh well… I'm reminded of the batik class I took at Palfrey; sure gave me perspective on how complex the process is!

After prayers – which were nice-sounding – although there was no wool spinning as at Hemlatta's school, I sat in the library for a short time and looked at a couple of books. Then I joined Varsha and her friend for tea and read "The Tin Drum" as they corrected entrance examinations, which were in English, Gujarati, Hindi, and Maharati – got to hand it to the teachers dealing with four languages!

Another wonderful meal at Hemlatta's. I find it strange to be served alone in the living room as the esteemed guest. Only after I finished did Hemlatta, her mother-in-law and Roopa sit down on the kitchen floor to eat. Strange custom.

Tomorrow I will go to Hemlatta's school at 3:00 PM. I will accompany Archana's two sisters to their home for dinner which should prove interesting. Hemlata has asked me to play flute for the 10th and 11th graders on Saturday morning – as there's going to be some sort of special program. Damn – I haven't played in ages so I've got some practicing to do tomorrow! "Hatikva," "Eli, Eli" – maybe "Bourée."

I don't know about my health again – my stomach hasn't felt right today. I will go to Hemlata's school, and to Archana's home, but not to eat dinner. Damn… now I'm worried all over again that I'll have a relapse just as I was beginning to feel better.

(Journal) Friday February 28 - 8:15 pm

Went to Dr. Desai and brought Roopa to her Grandma's. The doctor told me that my dysentery had nothing to do with the hepatitis and he immediately accused me of eating the wrong foods… Damn – that meal Hemlata served me… He gave me 6 tabs of something like mexaform along with a bottle of light brown thick goop with a bland taste. He told me to abstain from sugarcane juice, barley water and fruits, although I could have apples – and of course rice and dal are okay.

Went to Hemlata's school at 2:30. She's a strange one – I don't like her very much. I actually think she's a jerk, though I know she's well-meaning. She always says "welcome" when I walk in – and then tends to ignore me. Anyway. I took a taxi, along with Archana's two sisters and small brother to the Santa Cruz railroad station. Once there we had to walk for five – ten minutes to their apartment. It's really nice with a VERY large living room, bedroom for the parents, one for the three girls, and one for the grandmother who is such an obese, ugly-looking woman! Well – of course I was offered everything under the sun to eat and drink. Indians piss me off the way they're always so insistent. I was practically forced to eat some sugarcane, a dish of sliced apples, some chocolate (didn't mind that at all – Amul chocolate is the best, and it was cold!) and then a piece of vegetable something or other.

After two hours of sitting during which we didn't have much to say, I asked Archana what she does besides her school work. She responded with "sewing, cooking…" my God I'd go crazy! I then asked her if she had any boyfriends. "No – when I'm 20 or 21 my parents will find a boy they like and bring him home to meet me. We will talk some, and then, if he likes me…" It really is like the dark ages.

[Archana went on to become a Homeopathic doctor. About eight or nine years after our meeting, she came to visit me at my rented apartment in San Francisco. I remember how odd it was accommodating a Jain with her strict vegan diet. She wouldn't even eat root vegetables based on the belief that they are living things… A few years after that I attended her arranged marriage to a Gujarati accountant who lived in Torrance, CA. Unfortunately we kept in touch and she wasn't very happy…]

So – at 5:00 PM we left and Archana took me to the Khadi Banisar which is a really small emporium in the busy Santa Cruz bazaar. I bought a Rajasthani door decoration piece. Archana wanted to pay for it (15.25), and when I insisted that she shouldn't, she bought me a small batik silk scarf which I'd been admiring for 12.10 Rs. Sometimes Indians can be too damn forceful making me feel so ridiculous and helpless!

Then I took a taxi back and walked to Dr. Desai, Jr.'s (the dentist) who took an x-ray and then drilled until he got out the bit of excess silver that's been bothering me. It's tender now and will hopefully feel fine by tomorrow. I really am lucky to be in Bombay, having all these medical problems. Feels good to be so well cared for!

As yet I haven't received any mail here (mail is delivered twice daily). I hope to hear from David tomorrow!

(Journal) Friday, March 1

Already? In five days it'll be five months since I left home. I admit to wishing I were headed there now as I'm feeling very homesick. Soon enough… meanwhile, I recognize that this is an amazing experience so I will continue to enjoy it as much as I can! I am so grateful for these kind, hospitable people who are caring for me so graciously. It's fun that they refer to Dad as "Dr. Paul" and they revere him for taking care of their beloved family in Boston!

Today passed pretty uneventfully with the exception of those damn dysentery cramps this morning. Dr. Desai gave me more of the Pepto-Bismol-like stuff saying this has nothing to do with the jaundice – that I'm cured of that. But I've got to watch my diet… I just wish I felt better.

I went to Juhu beach by taxi with Hemlata, Padmaja and her friend Neeta's younger sister. I love the beach… We watched the sun melt into the sea; such a lovely time of day with pleasant temperature, a slight breeze making the palms ruffle. Met 3 Krishna-consciousness sisters from a temple at Juhu that I hope to visit one of these days.

Ate supper at Hemlata's again, and once more there were too many spices. I refused to eat the spinach and noodle mixture which, though it tasted good, was spicy and oily. I know I'm hurting feelings by turning food away, but damn, it's my stomach!

Again no letter from David – or from home. I wonder if he's even written? And when he's coming back to Bombay? It seems like ages ago that we said, "See you soon." Hopefully he'll be here in 3-5 days. I can't wait!

(Journal) Sunday, March 3

At around 11:00 this morning I was eating lunch at Hemlata's and Grandma called to say David had arrived! Yay! So Hemlata packed a lunch for me to bring him in the Indian style stainless steel containers with four layers on top of each other. There's a handle and it's about a foot and a half high.

Absence sure does make the heart grow fonder! David and I are happy to reunite. After we drank tea, and David ate, we headed for town. On the train I met Droffey Traynor, a Catholic Indian (!). She's 19 and is a stenographer on her way to the Regal Cinema to see *The Crazy Boys in the Games*, and we were headed for the Sterling Cinema to see *The Party* with Peter Sellers. She had her cab drop us off at the Sterling, as it's on the way. She gave me her number so I will call her and perhaps we will visit her home. It's fun to meet other people my age.

Since it's Sunday when all the locals go out, both the 3:30 and 6:00 shows were sold out and the 9:00 PM show would be too late, so we decided to go back to see the movie on Tuesday.

We went to Dipti's and met Hans, with whom David spent all week in Goa (they'd come back to Bombay together by boat). There were many people selling beautiful Rajasthani things but for such high prices. I really loved one wall hanging which would be perfect for over a door, but the woman asked for 250 Rps. She finally came down to 200 yet refused to budge lower and it was still too expensive for us. Perhaps it'll still be there and she'll change her mind in a few days.

Then the 3 of us went to the Indian Arts Demonstration near Churchgate. Beautifully set up displays of goods from Kashmir, Rajasthan, Uttar Pradesh, etc. There was a ferris wheel, camel and pony rides, lots of eating and drinking. Having to control my diet is such a pain in the neck because so much of the Indian diet consists of fried foods. Out of so many beautiful things, all I ended up buying was a silk batiked tie for Dad and David bought a good dictionary. He is really serious about wanting to teach English in Iran.

So, tomorrow morning we will fulfill our promise and play our flutes at Hemlata's school, then go directly to Churchgate to the tourist office to inquire about getting to Delhi re: the price by air, etc. Maybe they'll be able to get us train reservations without our having to wait 10 days… Then there's so much else to do. Bombay is a great place to buy things. We will go to the Bindy bazaar and back to the silver bazaar – and I'm determined to buy some Rajasthani things. I love the mirrored pieces. Anyway – enough writing for now. Goodnight. My boredom is over now with Dave here and so many things to do. Glad my health is good (no more shits!) but I'll continue to eat really carefully.

(Journal) Tuesday, March 5

We picked up our student concessions and went to buy tickets. I waited in one line, David in another. The trains go to Patna. The one David inquired about was free only on the 6th and 14th – tomorrow is too soon and the 14th is later than we want to leave. I finally got to the front of my line (after 2 hours including the 1/2 hour lunch break!) but the guy said our concession (discount coupons) was wrong or something. Dave tried to kill a few birds with one stone, and got student concessions for Bombay-Patna, Patna-Raxaul, Raxaul-Patna, Patna Armritsar all at once. Then we were informed that we'd have to purchase all

INDIAN HOSPITALITY IS THE BEST! : BOMBAY

the regular price – 139 Rs. for two seats – god-damn rip-off!

Oh boy… Today I flipped out. I simply couldn't help myself and started yelling at the guy who was giving us a hard time about our concessions/coupons being wrong. Sometimes I just have no control over myself. Not feeling well added to it, but I guess I just shouldn't be here. I am thinking that maybe everything Mom and Dad told me was right; that this just wasn't the time in my life for me to travel. That I should just have gone to college… that I just wasn't ready for a trip like this; not mature enough for it. I'll never have tolerance for all

the tickets at once, or some such bullshit – damn! To make a long, very frustrating story short, we realized that we'd have to get another concession, which meant waiting yet another day, risking our chances at getting a reservation before who knows when. So, fed up, we paid the bureaucratic bullshit one has to put up with in this country. My temper... I don't know why I can't control it. Part of me is saying, "Hold your tongue. Shut up," but the other part wants to – feels the need to – release the tension. Never have I been able to suffer quietly. I always complain – even when I know I should shut up. The spoiled, ugly and loud parts of me blurts it all out. It's like there are two forces within me always arguing – tearing ME apart, making me feel sad. Sad about myself and confused. David loves me... why? I must turn over a new leaf. I imagine we'll be splitting up shortly and don't want it to be on bad terms.

I'm envious of David – of the fact that he's able to be himself all the time – no matter what, and that he's able to be happy no matter what. He's so patient, understanding, undemanding, sympathetic, wise, experienced... It's beautiful how he tries to help me to help myself. I don't know, I'm having a rough time getting my head together...

Saw *The Party* which was just as funny as I remembered. Actually, even funnier, because Peter Sellers played an Indian from Bombay in the movie and does such a good job with a perfect accent! I needed that laughter so... great release after such a stressful day.

(Journal) Wednesday, March 6

Such an interesting day. We hung around all morning, then walked to Vile Parle East to buy English grammar books for Dave. What a market! I'll have to look around that section of town sometime soon.

Then we met Dr. Desai and he drove us to their "modest" home?! A three story house. First we sat in the living room drinking Fanta, and looked at his eldest son's wedding pictures. So much pageantry involved! Pretty interesting. When a Hindu is born, his horoscope is plotted by a priest – and before marriage the two horoscopes must be compared to see if the couple are compatible.

Dr. Desai showed us the amazingly long, intricate scrolls written in Sanskrit. He told us all about the Gods and showed us a brass platter with a carving of Shiva. I never knew that the flow of water spurting from Shiva's head represents the flowing of the Ganges River. And every Hindu has a sealed container of water from the Holy Ganges so when a family member is on his death bed, some of this water is placed in his mouth along with a leaf or two from the holy Tulsi Plant which every Hindu has growing in or outside his home. He showed us the rest of his home: upstairs is Hemlata's room which is modern with a huge bed, tape recorder, clock and a beautifully clean blue enameled western-style bathroom which was so refreshing to use. Never knew how spoiled we are to toilets!!! Dr. Desai claims that they had the bathroom made to accommodate the westerners they occasionally entertain. Then he showed us the roof with the garden below including the breadfruit tree – finally I know what breadfruit looks like!

Then we walked to the train station via an amazing market. We said good-bye. He really is sweet – though a bit spaced out, but so nice and generous with his time.

We took the train to Santa Cruz and walked the 5 minutes or so to Archana's home. There we had coffee and sat around talking with her two younger sisters ages 12 and 14 and their adorable 6-year-old brother who looks so much like Davy Mittel. We visited her cousin's home – same building – and of course we're invited to dinner.

Thursday, March 6 - 9:00 am

Howdy!

I can't believe how stuffed I am from last night's dinner! We were invited to the home of one of Hemlata's students (Hemlata is one of Dr. Shah's five sisters and lives with him). Her name is Archana – she's 15 and in her last year of school. In June she will begin college. In India children go to school when they're 3 – spend 2 yr. in kindergarten and then eleven years in school. When we were playing our flutes, Archana came running up and asked me if we could please exchange addresses – and would I PLEASE come to her home. Well, she is the oldest of 4, has two sisters aged 14 and 12 – and an adorable brother who looks amazingly like David Mittel – aged 6. Her father was born into a very wealthy family and inherited the family building contracting companies; one of the largest in Bombay. He's traveled through Japan, Malaysia, Singapore – and he and his wife (who speaks no English unfortunately) are planning a trip to the states – probably this summer. They have Indian friends living in Wisconsin who write home saying they're freezing.

We arrived at 6:30 and were served coffee. We sat around discussing religion; they're Jains – strict vegetarians who pray to a living Guru – and to 25 Gods. Jainism has nothing to do with Hinduism (I wish to read up on Jainism – it sounds fascinating – originating around the same time as Buddhism.) Anyway – dinner was served at 8:30 or so. As is Indian custom, guests are served first while the family waits until we're completely finished. Every time I'd take a bite or two of anything – my plate would be piled high with more. It's impossible to say no to any Indian, they just don't understand! The trick is to fast two days in advance. Friday night we're going to Archana's cousin's house (next door) for dinner. Everyone we meet invites us for dinner! As you've probably guessed, I've gained weight; inevitable here! And I had been in pretty good shape for a while (if I do say so myself) – it's the home-cooking – and lack of exercise – the heat makes it difficult to do too much running around – and every day is hotter than the day before... and so humid! Miserable climate, if you ask me – I can't wait to head north to Nepal and the mountains where it will be way more comfortable!

We have reservations for the 8:00 PM train (March 10) to Patna. 36 hours – yuck – but it won't be so bad – as we have reserved upper berths in a 3-tiered sleeper car. This means we'll get two nights' sleep and only have one day to suffer through... Then from Patna we'll fly to Kathmandu for only about $18 each (with the 25% youth fare deduction). At the airport's duty free shop we'll buy some liquor and other stuff that's really cheap and we'll sell it in Kathmandu and make back some of the money! I'm so glad you got that package as I never thought it'd get there! And I do hope Jeri likes the shirt... I really liked the embroidery.

David is studying up on English grammar and vocabulary as he is very seriously considering getting a job tutoring English in Iran. We've heard that there's a very high demand particularly for Americans as so many of Iran's young people wish to study in the US and UK – and now have plenty of $ with which to do so. The pay for English teachers is good.

Love, Karen

(Journal) Friday, March 7

We're now beginning our 6th month on the road. Yesterday we went into town – and to the Bindy Bazaar. Bombay really is amazing – just so vast! What a market!! Street after street bustling with humanity, people selling everything in unbelievable quantities! So crowded... In the Muslim section of town all the women are fully covered by chaderies (burkhas) and the

mostly bearded men are all intense-looking (I hate the way they stare at me and wish David would stay closer by my side while we walk around). Many perfume shops all in a row, and optical stores – or rather, stands with men selling sunglasses they have displayed all over their bodies. And food of all sorts: dried fruits on carts including figs, dates, raisins, cashews… Cows, horses, goats – huge veggie markets – and meat markets – and buses and taxis – and chai shops and restaurants – and clothes for sale – shoes – sandals. We wanted to find pouches like the ones Stuart and Gary have – well – on a little side street there was stand after stand of pouches – along with household goods such as spoons, etc. We stopped at the 1st stand – as there was a good selection. After 1/2 an hour we chose 59 pouches. They really are nice, and I'm sure we'll get a good price for them at home. Today we will post our package – all the pouches (except 2), the old Rajasthani piece I bought, the silk scarf Archana bought for me – the over-the-door decoration piece – silk tie for Dad – and the mirrored vest from the Khadi Emporium – so.

Midnight

After yet another great meal we arrived at Archana's at around 6:30 pm. Archana is such a love. It's hard to believe she's only going to be 16 on the 9th of April! So mature…

After Dave and I took turns playing the flute Archana took me into her room to talk. She wanted to know my plans. She showed me how to wrap a sari – there are two ways – Bengali and Gujarati – using the beautiful sari she's in the middle of embroidering. I promised to write her from Nepal, and to send the pouches (and some stamps for her cousin and youngest sister).

After dinner Archana's parents came over. We all sat around for awhile, then said our good-byes. Along with Archana's whole family we climbed into Mr. P.G. Mehta's Ambassador (1962) and were driven home. Crazy drivers, these Indians!… It was so sad saying good-bye to Archana; I hope we'll meet again someday…

So – we arrived "home" at around 10:30-10:45 to find no one here. The door was padlocked so we knew there was some sort of trouble since it was too late for everyone to be out taking a walk. So we went for tea, and when we came back Mukesh, Roopa, and Auntie (the same one who was here when I first came) were here and informed us that Mukesh's uncle died today. This afternoon his (Mukesh's) mother had told me he was sick… death is so difficult to accept. A black cap is hanging on the wall in "our" room.

Saturday, March 8 – 8:20 am

Good morning,

It's so pleasant at this time of day – too bad in a couple of hours it'll be so hot and humid! I'll be glad to head northward on Monday. On Thursday we went into town and to the Bindy bazaar, in the Muslim Section of the city. Street after street of bustling humanity – I've never seen so much happening at one time! Anything you could ever think of, and it's available to buy.

Today, we're taking the camera into town. I just realized that we've been here awhile and I've become very accustomed to all the things I write about. But you people would be fascinated to see it all so we'll return to that bazaar and take pictures of all the different kinds of people selling their various things – and maybe we'll ride on the top of a double-decker bus for a different perspective of Bombay! Also – we're going to visit the Aquarium in Bombay which I doubt is anywhere as great as the one in Boston, but we shall see.

It's going to be difficult to say good-bye to these people who've been so kind and generous. I'm sure that nowhere in the world could people be more hospitable than in India. I only hope that someday some of them will come to Boston and I will be able to show them around and return their hospitality. Can you imagine going into a clothes store, or a post office at home and be served tea? That's always the case here! And such good tea it is with milk and cardamom. I'll miss Indian food and their style of eating with their hands! But I won't miss India… As much as it's a fascinating place to visit and I don't for one minute regret having come, the extremes are getting to me. And, everyone should see this part of the world as it's amazing!

Love,
Karen

Sunday, March 9 - 10:00 pm

Howdy,

I'm really finding it hard to believe that tomorrow night at this time we will be en route to Patna – aboard a lovely Indian train. It shouldn't be too bad a ride since we have sleeper reservations. We requested upper berths to be above everyone.

I feel like I've been here in Bombay for ages though it's only been two and a half weeks. Oh, and a week before we went to Goa as well. I am overwhelmed by the hospitality of Dr. Shah's family and the many people we've met through them. We've both had to see a dentist so a Dr. Desai was suggested. He just graduated (1st in his class) from a leading school of dentistry in Bombay, and was awarded an honorary degree by the American Society of Dentistry for Children. He really seems competent and explains everything he's doing. He did a great job putting a gold crown on one of David's teeth and it only cost 50 rupees! Each silver filling costs only 10 rupees. Luckily I've had no new cavities, though have lost half of two fillings. Anyway, he's a really nice guy. His father is a doctor (general practitioner) and his mother works with him. His older brother is an engineer and lives in Poughkeepsie, NY with his Indian wife, who is expecting at the beginning of April. So Mrs. Desai will be flying to NY on March 20. Anyway, we were invited for tea the other day. They live in a house surrounded by high schools. They had it built there when their sons were young so they'd be near school. Dr. Desai (senior) showed us all sorts of photos: the boys growing up, his elder son's wedding – such pageantry in the Hindu religion! I've learned so much about Indian culture since I've been in Bombay. The Shah's family are Gujaratis and we've been able to observe the way Roopa's grandmother prays every morning. She sings and chants, making offerings of fruit and flowers to the family God plus to Lord Krishna (God of Life) and Shiva (the destroyer). We've eaten Gujarati food and Hemlata, (who teaches at the school I wrote about) has been wonderful. Today we ate lunch with her and afterwards she dressed me up in a gorgeous red and white silk batiked sari with a white blouse. She braided my hair in a single braid as the Indians do, put a gold necklace and a black dot on my forehead and had David take a couple of pictures. One of me alone, one of Roopa, me and Padmaja (Hemlata's 5 yr. old daughter). I even wore the sari into town! They really are comfortable! Although I felt really awkward as I felt so dressed up! But I certainly did fit right in which was wonderful!

And while Dhana's been away – another sister (don't know her name) has been staying here with their mother and Roopa. She speaks no English, but has been so kind to us and is such a great cook! I'm really going to miss Gujarati cooking. It's sweet and spicy and I love eating with my hands using chapattis. I only wish I could cook like these people! I've tried to learn by watching, but so many spices are tossed into everything – it's impossible to remember, especially since I have no idea what they are!

It's going to be very sad saying good-bye, knowing I'll probably never see most of these people ever again. Today, I took pictures of Neeta's family (Neeta is the 22 yr. old girl living with the Shah's). Her family is great. I love her mother, even though she speaks no English. I feel very close to her as she's so warm; holds my hand whenever I see her. I almost cried saying good-bye to her. Most of all I will miss little Roopa. I've had lots of fun with her; taught her lots of English. She can identify just about all the body parts and loves to sing "Where is Thumbkin." She can't say "pointer" and "pinkie" but pronounces the "p" as "f" "fointer" and "finky". She's so cute! And I think she'll miss me a lot, too. We've spent a lot of time together. I'll miss the way she calls me Keden ben (Karen sister) and comes running to be picked up… bet she won't even recognize me when I see her in the states.

Yes, this has been a home away from home – an oasis. I have been away a really long time at this point, and I am very homesick. But before heading home I must see more of Nepal!

I anticipate being home sometime this summer. After Nepal I think I will go to Kashmir, possibly to Darjeeling and Sikkim. Then we'll probably fly to Europe and fly home. Over land is tiring and time-consuming although it is much cheaper. Dave wants to earn more money so he may continue traveling for a while longer. There are some people who are content and fulfilled traveling all the time. I'm not one of them, as I feel the need to go home and study and help people… although I can't condemn Dave because I know he is a very happy person – doing what he wants – I'll have to work for my fulfillment – and I'm prepared to do so.

Love,
Karen

INDIAN HOSPITALITY IS THE BEST! : BOMBAY

(Photograph) Sunday, March 9

Bombay – I'm a bit pale, but at least you know what I look like in a sari! The Shah's family dressed me up on my last full day there, and made me go into town! It's a beautiful silk red and white batik.

Love, Karen

(Journal) Monday, March 10

The train departed Bombay Station at 7:40 PM, and now we're en route to Patna. We didn't get the upper tiers we asked for. Instead we're numbers 17 and 24 – next to the window. Oh well… this train is pretty grungy but there's some really nice people: a man from Poona; a train mechanics supervisor on vacation. I guess he gets his train fares paid for, so he really takes advantage and is traveling with his adorable 2 1/2 yr. old son. They're headed to Kathmandu, where they will stay only a couple of days.

When Mukesh told Roopa we were leaving (by that time I was crying) and I kept saying "Roopa ben," but she refused to look at me. Then she told Mukesh to prepare our bed. He again explained that we were leaving and wouldn't be coming back. She said she wanted to come to my house. I reached for her, but she wouldn't let me touch her. Instead she thrashed out at me so angry – justifiably so. Then she took a hanky and dried my tears and said, "Bye-bye". Then David was crying, and Mukesh was as well… they walked us downstairs and stood waving 'til we were out of sight. We realized we'd forgotten the water container so after walking for only five minutes we turned around… David ran upstairs and Mukesh said Roopa was asking where we were going and she was still sobbing. I already miss that little cutie. I wonder if she'll recognize me when I see her in Lexington? Maybe showing her pictures will remind her… I'm overwhelmed by the hospitality of the entire family and their friends. I'm sure that nowhere in the world would people extend themselves like this; I hope that someday some of those beautiful people will come to Boston and it will be my turn to welcome them – give them a home away from home.

(Journal) Wednesday, March 12 - 8:15 pm

Twelve hours ago our train pulled into Patna. Happy to say the railroad station scene wasn't at all heavy. We took a rickshaw directly to the Royal Nepalese Airlines Office – to find out that it was impossible for us to fly today, as they were all booked up. We bought tickets for

tomorrow's 10:30 AM flight. We saw Ashok and Angie (Dave had met them on the boat from Goa). He's Nepalese and she's English. They invited us to his "flat" just near Freak Street. They flew to Kathmandu today after having to spend four days here waiting. I guess there's been quite an influx of tourists following the coronation – hope the city won't be too crowded!

From what I've seen of Patna, it doesn't seem as poverty devastated as I had expected. As a matter of fact, not a single beggar approached me, although every rickshah walla and shoeshine boy tried to get double the price from us. I always feel like such a pig – paying the poor, rag-bedecked skinny little guy a rupee 50 Np. each – for peddling us around for 10-15 minutes. David gives what he feels is the price – always much lower than I think. Today we argued… I know he's right. If we give more than the price – it screws it up for other tourists.

I can't believe I'll be in Kathmandu before noon tomorrow!

HITCHHIKING TO KATHMANDU: MY OVERLAND ODYSSEY, 1974

CHAPTER THIRTEEN

DROPPING IN WITH THE LOCALS

KATHMANDU

(Journal) Friday, March 14

Didn't make it to Kathmandu before noon, as the plane was delayed until 1:30. But we managed to have a good time at the airport where they served us a light lunch. There we met Jessica, 29 years old and Jewish from New York. But she's now into Tibetan Buddhism and is here visiting her Rimpoche lama, apparently believing she was a Buddhist monk in one of her past lives. It's so hard to understand, never mind explain. Intriguing, unbelievable, fantastic… yet, somehow I do believe her though she's extremely spaced out, annoyingly so.

The 40-minute flight was great. I sat in the front row though sadly not next to the window. The plane was a 30 seater with seats on each side of the aisle. We were served Carlsborg Export beer which was really nice.

Dave got as buzzed as possible, more than 5 cans I think! The Himalaya rose like a white cloud on the horizon steadily forming into unique peaks, with Mt. Everest, the highest

mountain in the world and the only mountain with a cloud above it.

Landing in Kathmandu was such a rush; I'm so happy to be back here!!! At the airport in Patna we met Jerry Christian, an amazing French man around 35. He's big – fit stomach – funny as anything and he works as a translator in Paris. He speaks French, Bulgarian (his original language), Spanish, Portuguese, English, German, Turkish. Amazingly enough, he's Armenian (name was Kevorkian!) and speaks Armenian with David.

We went straight to The Oriental Hotel where we took a triple room for Dave, me, and Jessica. Jerry took a room next door. We got our packs, which had been safely stored. I'm totally disgusted with all the totally ridiculous, superfluous bullshit I "possess." This process of elimination is a total pain in the neck!

Kathmandu looks beautiful; I can't believe the change since we were here. They renovated the city so fast! Every pagoda and temple has been repaired and painted, new sidewalks, newly paved streets – there are even new facades for stores – especially on Gorga Path. It's nice to see many familiar faces.

Then we walked all over the bazaar as all the temples were lighted looking so beautiful. The lights are in honor of the coronation, but the people wished for them to remain. They are only lit on Friday and Saturday as well as for holidays and festivals.

David will be leaving for the Annapurna sanctuary to join an Austrian climbing expedition in a couple of days, as soon as he finds a climbing partner. I've decided not to join him. First of all, I wish to find myself a meditation teacher as I must begin to look within – or shall I say – from within. I need to be alone, to retreat for awhile, to take time to straighten out my confusion. I want to become more calm. I must collect my emotions and sort them out with care… it will seem strange being here alone.

(Journal) Sunday, March 16

A month from today, I'll be nineteen years old and next year, I'll be 20 …

Dave's really getting his shit together for his expedition. He spoke with his Sherpa friend who's the guy who brought a rope to us at the Annapurna Lodge before we went to Helambu – then we saw him that day we climbed up and over the 15,100 foot pass. Anyway, the head Sherpa from the Sherpa society opened a new place near the PO. He's letting David rent two ropes, gaiters, pitons, goggles, snow seal, windbreaker pants. Now all David needs is two climbing partners – he's left notes at the Kathmandu Guest house and a few other places.

So I'll find myself a nice room somewhere. I'd love to be in a place with a garden but the Kathmandu Guest House is all filled. Maybe there's a waiting list? I look forward to spending time alone. And I've found out that I should go to Bodhnath, that I'll be able to find a meditation teacher there. I'm feeling better lately, less lonely, as I begin to meet people here. Ashok and Angie and Jane who was on the plane with us. She's staying at "The Camp" hotel and says it's very peaceful. I'm at Eat at Joe's now.

Sunday, March 16

Hello!

I'm a bit more settled now than I was when I wrote that other letter as I've been meeting a lot of really interesting people here. The other night I ate dinner with two guys from Boston – one of them went to the Cambridge School in Weston a few years ago, and his friend looked very familiar to me. I think I waited on him at Charlie's Beef and Beer in Somerville. It's a small world!

Last night Dave and I visited Angie and Ashok – he's Nepali and she's English. They live in a small apartment. Ashok runs a small curio shop, and Angie is trying to organize some sort of a home for the 10 or so orphans (boys) who live on Freak Street. It really is sad to see them dressed in their torn clothing, asking for paisa. I try to give food to at least one of them every day – last night I split my sweet and sour vegetables and plain rice with a little boy. None of them are starving because tourists like me see that they get food.

But the poor little kids sure seem love starved. One orphaned 8-year-old boy in particular pulls my heartstrings. When I was in Kathmandu last December he was dressed in dirty rags, always coming to me, reaching to hold my hand. His eyes are dark and sparkly, and he seems very intelligent, speaks English well. He was quick to tell everyone he has no

parents... Anyway, one day in Pokhara, I saw the same little boy wearing a whole new set of western clothing. Clean face, shiny shoes, and a big smile. A French man (who is a Buddhist monk with a shaved head and wearing maroon robes) had taken him under his wing, and was trying to find a place for him to live in a monastery in Pokhara. But unfortunately there were already 2 or 3 orphans living there, and monasteries are VERY poor, so the boy is back in Kathmandu again, back on Freak Street. He says he's living in a temple here in Kathmandu, but I always see him on the street now asking for food. And because he's dressed, he's entitled to enter restaurants. Oh, I do wish I could take them all under my wing. I've decided that when I'm ready to take the responsibility of raising a child, that child will come from a third world country…

Our money is running kind of low. We've asked Vicki and Ellen to bring us $350 cash, but we're not sure if they will. So I'd love for you to send me $400 from my account. I've spoken with many other Americans about the best way to have money sent. It seems that the quickest and surest way is through Nepal Bank Limited. What you should do is go to an affiliate branch of Chase Manhattan Bank and have them wire the $400. It should reach me between 3-6 days from the time you send it. Nepal Bank Limited will issue me the money in the form of "First National City Bank" travelers' cheques. I would love it if you'd send me a telegram when you receive this letter so I'll know when to expect the $. Send the telegram c/o American Express, Yeti Travels, Kathmandu, Nepal. Thank you!

Kathmandu is so beautiful now that it's been redone for the coronation. All the temples and pagodas are lit up. We're trying to recharge our flashlight that was ruined by a rainstorm in Greece. Finally we found someone with a charger: a professor of psychology from Illinois.

Well, David is very seriously preparing to climb Tent Peak (18,500 ft.), which is in the center of the Annapurna Sanctuary. He's now making himself snowshoes out of bamboo! He's put ads up for two experienced climbers. I hope he finds someone because he's so excited; getting everything together, exercising every morning as it will be a difficult climb; quite the challenge – even dangerous I hear. I don't like that part – makes me nervous. I will either find myself a nice quiet hotel room or a room out toward Swayambhu. I heard that there's a meditation course (transcendental) being given about 15 minutes away from here. I will investigate that tomorrow morning, and then I'll let you know what I'm doing.

In a couple of days we're going to take a day's trek. We'll take a bus to Bhadgaon (in Kathmandu Valley), and then walk up to Nagarkot, from where there's a great view of the high Himalaya – even Everest, which is pretty far away! Time really is nonexistent in Nepal – such a lazy pace – one gets side-tracked so easily while in the city. It takes a long time to get things done so I hope to receive a telegram and I didn't send one because I've heard bad reports that they take longer than letters!

Love and miss everyone,
Karen

(Journal) Monday, March 17

A letter from the sisters on the farm. Caroline… she writes so beautifully – sounds happy – and Heather, Sid, and Boe… I was a little saddened by their letter because it made me realize that when I get home everything's going to be different: friendships, people change with time, and experiences – "slipping away" – Caroline and friends are so far away and into such different trips. Different from each other – and from me especially. How can I explain a trip to the East??

I was disappointed not to hear from Mom and a bit surprised, too. I don't know why I can't seem to get things together; still don't know what to do. We'll probably trek to Ghorapani, which is as far as the Jomosom trek, altogether about ten days from Pokhara. As for the meditation – I just don't know what's happening. For the time being Dave is here still trying to find someone to climb with.

(Journal) Wednesday, March 19

Last night we went to Ashok and Angie's with spaced out Jerry. He was hopped up on Dexedrine, then smoke, then rum and cokes. I danced for the first time in ages to The Who's rock opera *Tommy* which sounded good. It felt great to move! I do need more exercise.

Looks like Ashok will get a passport, thanks to Jerry. They had no problem at the French embassy. Jerry really is a nice guy. He's so genuinely thankful to Dave and me for "showing him around." He keeps giving us all these things. So far he's given us each a choker, me a Tonga, Dave he's taken out to eat a few times, gave him material for dress pants (black), me a little bead, and tonight…! He went crazy tonight; gave me two Tibetan dresses. One in

cheap black cotton, the other in turquoise brocaded Chinese silk, 2 shirts, an apron, a scarf, mirrored shoulder bag, a woolen vest – which Dave will give to Vahan – the silk dress and both shirts to Cynthia – the black dress to his mother – I'm amazed…

March 20

Hello!

Kathmandu is a fantastic place. Today Dave and I rented bikes and rode out to Pushpatinath, the holiest temple (Hindu) in Nepal. Last week there was a Shiva festival (Shiva is one of the most important Gods – "the Destroyer"), and apparently, many, many Indians came to Nepal and to Pushpatinath to celebrate.

From the outside, the temple is beautifully painted and intricately carved and intriguing, but only Hindus are allowed to enter. They wouldn't even let us take a picture. But we were told to walk around to the other side of the village where we found ourselves amidst hundreds of temples, some only large enough for the small figurines of Gods, others large enough for a good number of people. The holy Bagmati River runs through, and we saw bodies being cremated upon stone ghats by the water's edge; and there's a large hill with temples all over. Trees, grass and monkeys everywhere! I've never seen so many.

And there's a "Baba" (a baba is a holy man or Sadhu as they're referred to in India) who wears a sarong, usually orange. His face is painted, and his hair, which he NEVER cuts or washes, is all matted looking like a bird's nest. Many of them are wanderers, nomads, Sadhus – they smoke chillums which are Eastern-style pipes, filled with ganja (marijuana) and they each carry a begging pot usually made of brass. They're the world's original hippies! Really, I've never been to a place so Eastern. Hinduism is such an intricate religion that I know so little about.

From the hill we saw that Boudhnath, the village from which we began our trek last December, was very close by. You see, there's a large stupa there. A stupa is a Buddhist temple that cannot be entered. It's painted gold with the eyes of Buddha painted on all four sides. So we rode to Bodhnath.

My plans are materializing. Dave has found a climbing partner (Fred) from Germany, so they are busy planning their climb. They'll probably start out around March 24, and it will take them 3 weeks. I plan to stay in Kathmandu for a little while – explore other parts of the valley, buy things and await the money I've asked you to send. I anticipate our being in Nepal through April. I'm going to trek to Ghoropani (10 days out of Pokhara), which is as far as the Jomsom trek is opened to. There's still trouble with the Khampa warriors near the Tibetan border. From Nepal we'll head to Kashmir and spend maybe a month there. From Kashmir, I will come directly home – maybe overland – although I think I will want to fly from Delhi to Europe and then use my return ticket from Munich to Montreal although I may fly from a different European city, as my ticket can be switched. I anticipate being home by July.

So, for a while still I'll be in Nepal. I love this mountain kingdom with its smiling people. No matter how built up Kathmandu and Pokhara become, the highlands will always remain the same due to their remoteness. All is peaceful here; I do hope the rest of the world never rubs off its ugliness upon Nepal. When I leave here, it will be with the thought in mind that someday I shall return, perhaps to work with the people. And I do hope all of you will someday visit Nepal!

Monday, March 24 - 11:00 am

It's 11:00 AM now, Monday, the 24th of March. We've just returned from two days and two nights of camping – 1/2 way between here and the Tibetan border. It was a culturally very interesting weekend.

On Saturday morning we put on our packs and walked up the street to the Mercedes Bus, with Fred, the guy with whom David will climb his Himalayan peak. Fred rode the bus overland from Germany; two Mercedes buses traveled together – one will be sold here, the other in Delhi, and the drivers will fly back to Germany, buy more buses, and start over again. This is their 5th trip. Anyway – there were twenty-six of us; about 8 German guys, a wonderful Swiss (German) couple, a French couple, an English girl, a guy from Vancouver with his Danish girlfriend, a French Canadian girl traveling with her three Spanish girlfriends with whom she worked in Switzerland, another Spanish woman traveling herself, a weird guy from Brazil who looked like an EXTREMELY absent-minded professor. He wore baggy, baggy pants which were tight down around his ankles and big boots and a spy-like shabby trenchcoat… Also, another Brazilian (NO connection between the two) 28 yr. old Maria who speaks English perfectly (she lived in Vermont for 1 1/2 yr. and spent weekends in Boston). She studied English at a very small school in Brattleboro, has lived in Australia, Malaysia, and various parts of Europe; a couple of Nepalis were with us, and one other American: Connie from California.

Anyway, as no one had anticipated more than 10-15 people, all was very disorganized.

Some food had been bought, but many of us thought that the driver would stop on the way to buy food, but the next thing we knew we were parking by a beautiful rushing river and setting up camp. Swimming, fishing (in vain), frisbee playing, getting to know people; was difficult at meal time – with any large group of people it's necessary to have a leader – a head cook – but there was no one in charge – no one who had dealt with large groups of people and knew what to do – so I kind of "took charge," but I found it very frustrating because it turned out that a lot of the people with us weren't very good people.

I took a local bus to a village where I could buy food. There wasn't much in the village. I bought over 50 eggs, 20 or so packs of glucose biscuits and tons of scallions – that's all they had – anyway – someone else bought bread in another town – so there was enough food for everyone to have two slices of bread and two eggs. But, while 1/2 the people were still sleeping, some people kept going back for seconds and thirds – I'd say, "You know, that's all the bread there is. Some people haven't eaten yet." But no one cared – the only reply I'd get would be a shrug – it made me sad – because of the lack of consideration… You know, I hate to generalize like this, but it seems that most of the many Germans I've come in contact with during my travels have been cold, arrogant, self-centered, loud-mouthed people.

But all in all, I managed to have a good time – diving off rocks into the deep freezing water – surfacing to find myself 10 yards downstream – and having to swim hard against the strong (but not overpowering) current to get to shore. And I found lots of pretty little wild flowers to put in my diary – it's looking good – I'm writing just about every day – flowers, pictures, designs – it's a beautiful red hard-cover book – canvas cover – found it in a back street bazaar in Bombay.

Now it's 9:30 AM on Tuesday – as usual, many distractions prevented me from finishing yesterday. David is leaving for Pokhara tomorrow. I will remain in Kathmandu for another 4 or 5 days, and then on to Pokhara. There I will begin my trek to Ghoripani, which is as far as the Jomosom trek is open. I'll meet up with David at Ghoripani around April 13 – and be in the mountains for my birthday – 19! Hard to believe! In a way I do wish I were home… Last night I dreamt about everyone – and that Mom sent me a birthday cake…

Anyway – love you all – hope $ is on its way – cuz we're running low… HAPPY SPRING!

Love, Karen

March 25 – 7:30 pm

Dear Grammy,

Today, I received your letter (the 2nd one in Kathmandu), and one from Dad – the carbon copy of the letter he wrote to Delhi – I can't tell you how happy I was and always am to receive letters!

I really do love Nepal. I've been exploring Kathmandu Valley, renting a bicycle for only three rupees per day (7:00 AM-6:00 PM). As I know I've mentioned to you before, here in Kathmandu, there's an excellent black market for dollars. As I walk down the street, western-dressed Nepalis (jeans, snazzy shoes – all have been given to them by, or brought from or traded with westerners) approach me, saying, "Change money madam? Very good rate today – you have cash dollars? For big bills we'll give you 12.65 rps. per $ – only 12.50 for $1 bills. $11.50 for cheques."

I've been reuniting with many friends – now we sit with Ulla and Ressu – Ulla is a beautiful fair-haired Finnish girl, and Ressu is her Swiss boyfriend, who speaks English as though he were from California! He also speaks German, Finnish, Russian, French, Spanish, and I think Italian. I went to eat a grilled cheese-tomato sandwich at a restaurant, and there, sipping glasses of tea, sat Ulla and Ressu! Such a coincidence, as they just arrived here in Kathmandu yesterday. I showed them around town – down to Assan Tole (street), a very busy bazaar street – but so much mellower than anywhere in India! The Nepalis are all smiling and fun to do business with, whereas I wouldn't be upset to never see an Indian again in my life – actually, that's a very unfair statement – yes I do hate India – but I love it, too – as I've said before and will say many more times – India is a land of extremes – very, very good – and horrible, yechhh, ugly, sad – intense! The hospitality of Dr. Shah's family overwhelmed me. I'm sure that nowhere in the world could people be kinder, but there's nothing uglier than the poverty and filth and the hassle and red tape one must go through when dealing with anything like train reservations, or banks, or post offices.

Today was really a nice day – was with Ulla and Ressu, reunited with two American guys (Calif.) with whom we ate a turkey dinner at X-mas time – they went to Darjeeling during the king's coronation. And I heard from you and Daddy and bought a weskit small vest. It's a tan background with little village scenes brocaded in light blue, green, brown, orange, and white – I love it! I spent an hour or so talking with Bob – an Australian guy we knew in Pokhara in Jan. – He's very intrigued by Tibet and its people. He is studying Tibetan – he has a Tibetan shepherd dog (1/2 wolf!!!), who has 5 (female) 2 wk. old puppies! Bob really has fascinating stories to tell about various places he's been – Grammy, it's time for sleeping – I do hope you will go to London or to Calif. – I agree – you should travel. I'm thinking of perhaps flying home from London – I've so many Eng. friends. I love hearing from you – stay well – you are amazing you know – shoveling snow – remain well!!!

(Journal) Thursday, March 27

David left for Pokhara early this morning – I cried a little; but I know it's good…

Spent the day with Angie; she's fed up with the way Ashok treats her possessively, selfishly, very inconsiderate – one-sided – and she has finally decided to fly home to London VERY shortly – it's really about time – don't understand how she could've taken so much shit for so long.

Well, we went to Swayambhu – met Ulla and Resso along the way; Ulla is so beautiful – we're sisters – but she really does feel inferior to Resso with his college education and knowledge of 7 languages. She's so ridiculously ashamed of wearing her glasses – feels they look just SO ugly – whereas they're all right, just a bit large – puts herself down for being nearsighted – and her eyes are less so than mine.

FULL MOON

Met Terry – sat around the Mandala – great supper of bread and cheese – played my flute – Terry played one of his bamboo recorder flutes, another guy tried the smaller one, and a guy from I don't know where, reminding me of Jono – also played bamboo flute.

From the Mandala we headed out to Balaju to a hotel which had a party happening. When we arrived, dinner was still being served; it turned out that the Danish couple who I think run the hotel were celebrating their marriage. When I walked in I was astonished – all westerners, fairly dressed up – felt like many "deja-vu's" – much dancing, an open bar – I had orange juices – and a delicious piece of cake.

At around midnight we – Terry, Jim, and I – left to walk back here to Kathmandu which took us about an hour. It was nice walking under the full moon.

March 27

Namaste!

Today is a beautiful sun-shining day – I sit upon the roof of my hotel looking out at Kathmandu Valley. The streets below me are full of laughing Nepalis throwing water balloons and colored powder at one another – and at unsuspecting tourists like myself – my hair's a lovely mixture of red and white powder. Today is the last day of "Holi," which is one of the major Hindu festivals celebrated in Lord Krishna's honor for 8 days. Tonight's the full moon – old and young alike are out having a great time!

So, I'm now staying at the "Mt. Everest Lodge." I have a large double room all to myself with two beds, cupboard, table and my own private balcony although I prefer to sit on the roof, as it's 3 floors higher, and affords such a wonderful view of the valley. Surrounded by small mountains and rolling hills; with the high white snow peaks in the distance – today obscured from view by fluffy white clouds. I can see the hill at Swayambhu – with the golden stupa at the top glistening in the sun. Tonight I will go climb the hill because it really is amazing up there when there's a full moon! Swayambhunath, the monastery next to the stupa, is the center of Tibetan Buddhism in Nepal. Always I see monks with shaved heads and maroon and orange robes, praying, actually, chanting – or sipping their yeccha tea – Tibetans drink tea mixed with yak butter – maybe up to 30-40 cups per day! I find it foul.

I'm now reading a fascinating book called *Tibet: Its History, Religion, and People* – written by a Tibetan monk – Thubten Tigme Norbu – who is the Dalai Lama's brother – Tibet is so intriguing! I'd love to go there – too bad it's not possible – but I have met many Tibetan refugees here in Nepal – how sad that people are driven out of their homeland.

And don't you like this card? The picture looks exactly like the place it's supposed to be, about 5 min. walk from here. Please save this (I know you always do) because I'd like to frame it.
 Karen

(Journal) Saturday, March 29

Finally I am reading *The Teachings of Don Juan* – wonderfully clear. Feeling really good lately, more peaceful. My temper is not apt to flare. I guess when I'm with one person a long time, I take out my frustrations upon them, but when they're not around I don't seem to have so many frustrations! Oh well…

Lately it seems as though I have far less problems than the people with whom I'm coming in contact! Poor Angie; she's so sweet, yet for so long has had her eyes shut – Ashok has been treating her horribly – more like a slave than a lover – as I've always felt; any relationship which is not TOTALLY mutual doesn't stand a chance – if it does continue, then it's only at the expense of the feelings of one of the involved individuals. Finally Angie is admitting to herself that she is worthy of a much more sincere relationship, that she doesn't have to put up with Ashok's bullshit any longer! How she could've been blind for so long I don't understand. I guess it's a common thing for people to build up false utopias within their minds. Of course originally, there must be a real basis. It's so sad that the kindest people are always getting their efforts thrown back in their faces…

Finished *The Teachings of Don Juan*. Incredible book – looking forward to *A Separate Reality*. I can't really say much about the book right now – in time, words will come.

(Journal) Easter Sunday, March 30

The sound of children laughing in the street below penetrated my soul with an inner gnawing – for nothing on this earth is more real – or more universal – how I love little ones!

When is it that inhibitions begin to darken young lives – taking away all joy – and an even more important question: Why is it almost inevitable that children must become conscious over every moment – unable to remain free and flowing…

Here in Nepal – away from the city, people have more of a chance of remaining free. I smile as I walk up the path to the music of little voices saying "Namaste," and wishing I could take hungry little beauties along with me – showing them that other sides of life really do exist – someday I will be doing my share.

(Journal) April 1

My last day in Kathmandu has passed. Spent the afternoon with Bob, Graham, and another Australian guy – amazing conversations about Alistair Crowley, author of *Book of Thoth* – I must read it. Also – *Record of Two Friendships* by Michael Serranno.

This morning I went to visit Angie – she's planning to head back to England shortly, though she will probably still be here when we return. Rented a duck down sleeping bag from AK. Something very upsetting has happened – Sir Edmund Hillary's wife and daughter were killed when their private plane crashed just outside of Kathmandu, 3 minutes from the airport en route to Solu Khumbu. Also, one dog, the New Zealand pilot, and two cousins of AK. He had to send a helicopter to bring Sir Edmund here from NZ – apparently he couldn't see the bodies – instead wished to sleep, after drinking some chang…(local rice beer)

Tuesday, April 1

Dear Grammy,

I can't believe today is April 1 and that in five days it will be six months since I left home… such a long time, yet it's gone by so very quickly. Tomorrow morning I am taking a bus to Pokhara, so I have so many things to do today! Buy a few things, such as toilet paper, shampoo, oranges, cheese – go to the bank and get a bunch of 1 rupee notes – as it's difficult to change tens in the mountains. By the way – Sunday I received Mom's telegram, and yesterday (Monday) I got the money! Absolute record time – only five days from Boston to Kathmandu! I have friends who've had to wait up to three weeks, and many telegrams never get through! Lately my luck has been very good – well, bad and good. I dropped my prescription sunglasses (which I'd had made in Delhi), and since they're made of glass, one lens broke. I went to an optician and he said I'd have to replace both lenses as he didn't have the right color – so I would have to pay 50 rupees – I went back to pick them up later and he said to only give him 25 rupees as he located the proper color! It's unbelievable how cheap everything is here – 25 rupees is under $2.50! For eye glasses! And my hotel bill for the last 5 nights came to only 35 rupees. Granted, it's no upper class hotel, but it's clean and there's lots of sun coming in and I have my own balcony.

Yesterday I went to the Air France office just to find out the costs of flights from Delhi to Europe. Today air prices are going up 8% worldwide! So there are no flights cheaper than $280. WITH youth or student deductions! That's really expensive, but I'm going to try and fly anyway. Some good friends of mine here in Kathmandu now are from Zurich. They're planning to be home at the beginning of June, so I may visit them before flying home. I'd really love to see some of Switzerland, and staying with friends would make it financially possible and a lot more enjoyable. But, as usual, I'm unable to let you know any definite plans, as I'm not sure yet myself. I am planning to leave Nepal during the first week in May – and go to Kashmir for 3-4 weeks. Kashmir is the only area in this part of the world which is not hit with an annual monsoon – except for the higher mountain regions, of course.

So – yesterday, I had a cholera booster shot – my arm's a little sore today – and I had another gamma globulin shot last week. Anyway – I must get on with some of the many things I have to do today – including saying good-bye to good, good friends…

Love you –
Karen

CHAPTER FOURTEEN

MY BIRTHDAY IN GHORIPANI ON THE JOMSOM TREK

POKHARA

(Journal) April 2

Alone… feeling somehow stronger and better able to cope. Goodbyes are so very difficult, and tonight I had to say it to 4 incredible people who I have come to love: Ulla and Ressu – it feels as though we've known one another for ages – they're so understanding. Ulla is so earnest, sweet, kind, considerate – more a sister than anyone else I've met during my journeys. Ressu, soft-spoken, very knowledgeable, a good friend who is so kind and considerate… Maybe we'll meet again here in May though perhaps our reunion will have to wait until someday when I'll visit them on their farm…

And Australian Bob – the most incredible man I've ever met! I love him. Every day for the past 2 weeks – especially since Dave left – I've spent time in his "home" in the Tibetan refuge camp on the edge of Pokhara. He really has moved in; his Tibetan tongas all over, little "kitchen," leather works spread about, and of course beautiful Kali with her 5 teddy bear puppies – 'cept for the runt of the litter. Poor little black and white creature so tiny and different from her sisters; really seems miserable…

And quiet Graham who is like a little boy; mysterious and suddenly disappearing so quickly. He's amazingly shy, withdrawn, always blinking, as if to hide for a moment… so sweet.

And Terry – spacey and sometimes too far away for me to follow, seems to live on a whole different plane – higher than mine (I haven't left earth yet!). Yet our minds flow evenly somehow – fine feelings – through both eye and body contact – such a beauty who's made an amazing picture for me on the next page of this journal.

This book shall ALWAYS be with me… Good-bye friends who I love – thanks for all of you being who you are – and where you are now – someday, our paths shall cross again…

(Journal) April 3

Such a pleasant day. Ed, Frank, and I rented a boat and paddled to the far end of the lake (myself being dead weight in the middle) where we stopped and I swam.

Lots of good people are around. Martin from Vancouver who I found where I left him in January, sitting outside at the Snowland, which of course hasn't changed a bit. Neither has the Bhatterhai where I sit now. I'm staying in a room near the Snowland for only 2 rupees per night. There are lots of animal noises at night, but I'll get used to them.

Missing David now – wonder how he is, where he is… shall be an incredible reunion in Ghoripani or somewhere on the trek!

New friends are filling voids – and old faces popping up. For example, Kathmandu faces; the French couple – she's blond and always wears a headband. Tonight was spent with Martin and Mark, who has also been here since before the coronation. In Krishna's house – Martin's staying there while Paula is in Kathmandu. Paula is amazing – so artistic. The house looks so clean – really a home with many pictures everywhere. She draws amazing fantasies – sorta like M.C. Escher – yet even more intense.

The three of us sat around talking for hours, and I played my flute. It feels so good to play! Really feel close to both of them, especially Martin. He reminds me of Chip sort of – his way of speaking and some little mannerisms. He'll be twenty in May but graduated a year early, so has already been to school for two years. There's just nothing like sitting around with friends – feeling totally myself, relaxed… Martin is so nice.

(Journal) April 4

It's oh so peaceful in Pokhara valley – but where are the mountains?? I haven't even caught a glimpse! Perhaps the haze will burn off.

Today Martin and I paddled across the lake and took turns reading Siddhartha aloud to one another. It's such a beautiful book – perfect surroundings for reading it! Pokhara is so incredible.

Peace pervades my being.

Margaret and Nils have arrived here in Pokhara today. They are staying next door at the Blue Star. We'll leave for trekking together on Monday.

April 4

Hello!

It feels so good to be back in Pokhara – it's so peaceful here. I'm sitting by the lake waiting for my coffee and French toast. The lake is incredibly refreshing, and the air is very warm, actually hot! So I go swimming at LEAST twice a day. Martin, a friend of mine from Vancouver, is still here in Nepal. He lived near us here in Pokhara in January. And Paula from San Francisco now lives in the house we lived in. She's an artist and has made such a nice home for herself. She's got a lot of money and has bought herself the most incredible stones – turquoise, coral, and Tibetan moonstones – over a hundred of them. I've never seen such a gorgeous necklace! And her artwork is somewhat like Escher, yet more intense – all done in pencil. Amazing work!

She has a tape deck with some tapes, and every other night the electricity is turned on so we go there and listen to music. Last night I played my flute for a few hours. I'm so glad I have it with me. Even though sometimes it does seem heavy, it's worth carrying. But I've tried to get into playing bamboo or wooden flutes, but they're just no fun compared to my beautiful silver open-holed Gemeinhardt.

These days I've just been relaxing, swimming, boating; lots of writing in my diary and pressing more and more flowers. My Australian friend Bob made a beautiful leather clasp for my book, which means so much to me, as I keep everything in there – letters, aerogrammes, flowers… I pray I'll never lose this book; I've lost two diaries already during this journey.

Unfortunately the weather hasn't been great. I've been here for two days now, and still haven't been able to see the mountain as it's been very hazy and yesterday was cloudy. Hopefully it'll clear by the time I go trekking which will probably be Sunday or maybe Monday. Tonight some friends – Margaret (Swiss) and her husband Nils (Danish) will be here. Hopefully we'll trek together – there's plenty of other people trekking to the same place – but I'd like to go with friends I've known for awhile.

I feel so at peace here in Nepal. Leaving will be very difficult especially not knowing when I'll be back… But I know I will be back someday, maybe to work with the Nepali people along some lines. There are many peace corps workers here – working in the Terrai (southern Nepal)… who knows?

David said that when he went through northern India in May two years ago, he saw at least three fights per day because people are just so uncomfortable in the intense heat and humidity. He took 3 cold showers with his clothes on every day just to feel a bit cooler. To tell you the truth – I don't care if I never see India again in my life! I am DEFINITELY planning to fly from Delhi to Europe.

(Journal) Saturday, April 5

I've been playing a lot lately; it feels so good here in Pokhara.

Today I was awakened (pre-dawn) by the sound of a huge water rat munching bread (which I'd left on the table like a dummy) right next to my head. He lumbered off as I saw that he'd chewed through the zipper on the top right side pocket of my pack; the bastard got at the soybeans in there. Zipper teeth and soy beans were scattered about. So I'm now staying in a room downstairs from where Kathy and Jeff stayed in the best house in town. Now, an English couple Neil and Wendy stay there. An amazing coincidence – Neil plays flute and has a silver (chrome) flute as does Jim (Colorado) who stays next door! I can't believe there are actually three silver flutes in one house and Dave's not even with us.

Tomorrow morning I shall walk to the end of the lake to find Gunter – I've heard he's staying in one of the 3 little houses at the end… wish to see him and to play with him as he is actually traveling with his guitar! Also, Martin's friend Robert plays guitar – maybe in the afternoon we'll get some music together.

All is pleasant – oh so timeless here in Pokhara. But I've been here four days and haven't caught even a glimpse of the mountains – it's been so hazy and cloudy and humid! But tonight it finally rained, and now the stars are out. I'm glad it's cooled off a bit. I've asked Jim to awaken me for the sunrise. I can't wait to see those majestic white peaks…

(Journal) April 6

Gunter…

Amazing day – awoke to see the sunrise – again, the mountains were enshrouded by haze! Sitting at the "Himalaya" and Gunter came by. We went to his house at the end of the lake. Very hot and muggy today! Swimming, sitting around… then playing incredible music. Really, never have I been so musically aligned with anyone – "Dona Dona" – nothing could sound more beautiful, and there was an audience of ten or so Nepalis sitting by the door.

Searching, searching – yes, so many of us are. Gunter is returning home very shortly – has less of an idea of what to expect when he gets there than I do. I'm able to understand him completely – to identify with him, to explain my thoughts.

(Journal) April 7

Awoke at 5:00 – left my extra stuff with the owner of my house, and headed for "The Blue Star" to meet Margaret and Nils for breakfast. Despite the hot day, I was wonderfully surprised to be able to see a bit of the mountains through the haze!

We headed out a little after 6:00 AM – stopped for chai and farewells at Gunter's… he's so beautiful – looking so deeply into my eyes – his eyes so blue. I wrote a bit for him – I know he'll always keep it… And he gave me this incredible ring – silver-design-engraved, swirly – with a milky orange stone. Its story is:

At Bande-Amir, a very old woman was sitting by a lake wearing many rings. She talked and talked to him. Gunter understood nothing but it didn't matter – many old people just feel good having someone who'll listen. Then she GAVE him the ring in gratitude.

Oh so hard to leave – just as a beautiful friendship was beginning – we make such incredible music together – never have I felt so high while playing – not even with Caroline at Palfrey.

Yes, good-byes are very painful but a very real aspect of life – yet they are inevitable. Perhaps someday our paths shall cross again.

It's 1:00 PM and I'm spending the hot hours of the day here at the top of the world – Pokhara Valley, anyway. Sunning, munching – so very high and peaceful. Flowers and friends – such amazing friends I've met during my travels like Margaret, who grew up in the Swiss Alps – and Nils – his mother is Norwegian, his father Danish. They're married and live in Zurich – working together, building scale models for large buildings, leading happy lives.

And now I lie in the middle of this enclosed field at the top of the hill – two Nepali girls by my side. How I wish there wasn't always the subject of baksheesh underlying every conversation – makes it difficult to make any REAL friendships.

An incredible number of butterflies and other insects – a hazy summer day that could be anywhere in the world. That is until one looks up at the stupendous Himalaya poking above the clouds!

At home with Margaret and Nils – feeling at peace. Lately, all has been good – doesn't matter really that a rat chewed up the zipper on one of the side pockets of my pack – or that my pack is heavier than I'd like for it to be – damn, it's worth it to have certain "comforts" of home with me – i.e. my sleeping pad. But how I wish I brought my flute rather than leave it – should've listened to Gunter!

Unfortunately, not even an inch of the mountains are showing through the clouds today although Macchapachure (fishtail mountain) showed its peak for a short while.

This is the place to go in order to enjoy trekking. It was worth climbing although for awhile I was seriously considering turning around as I just wasn't comfortable – but I know that in order to enjoy life, one must have to strive – to work – to feel that sense of accomplishment that makes it all worthwhile.

I fully understand all that my parents have said – although it wasn't a question of misunderstanding before – just not being able to admit to myself – always was aware deep down inside – although somehow I wasn't always able to keep my mind in one place at one time – spacing – unable to think about myself. But over the past six months, I've learned so very much. I've gained tolerance although my temper still "flashes". The only thing that will help me to overcome this fault, which I do consider very bad, is for me to get into some serious meditation, or yoga, which I will look into when I get home. It would be good to find a teacher in Nepal, but somehow it seems that while I am here in this part of the world, I should see as much as possible, as I can get into meditation anywhere although it's definitely time for me.

Our peaceful afternoon shattered when Harigaly stole my sunglasses. Spent 2 1/2 hours in Serencot, trying to get them back. It was obvious to the whole village that she had them, but still I wasn't able to get them back; police threatening and all – maybe on the way home I'll get them…

So sad that the people around here are so creepy – but I guess it's the fault of westerners. I love to give, but somehow I just can't when I'm being asked constantly.

Tuesday, April 8, 1975 - 6:45 pm

Chandracot is an incredible village high on a hill in an open windy valley. The hillsides look like great staircases, terraced to prevent the monsoon rains from washing away the top soil. Yellow fields of mustard flowers – or maybe it's saffron – all so lush and green. The houses with their thin thatched roofs and water buffaloes all around; I'll miss them with their clumsy bodies and tremendous horns – and they're so timid even though some are twice my size. And goats – the little babies so adorable – scampering gracefully up and down. Their cry sounds so human. And because it's spring, there are so many baby animals: fluffy calves, hairy buffalos, lambs… Today, walking up the trail, we passed three donkey (and mule) caravans. The animals all had bells, low and vibrating, and all were gaily decorated with feathered plumes and pom-poms.

from the spectacular, beautiful mountains – Macchapachure, with its fishtail enshrouded by opaque clouds. In the mornings it's so hazy – then clouds. And today there was thunder and a little rain, and the wind was so intense. For a while I had to wear my scarf over my face there was so much dust!

My God – never have I been in such a gorgeous place; it's surreal! Mountains everywhere, steep hillsides and those massive snow peaks! Annapurna seems so close! Foreboding. And

But now it's dusk, I sit here in Chandracot, tiny village with only six buildings, three of them restaurant/hotels for all the trekkers. The pink glow of the setting sun has faded now

the wind is so powerful I had to come inside. Winding rivers making their way up the valley, waterfalls, not gushing yet, as the snows are only just beginning to melt. In June, the rivers, streams, and waterfalls must be incredible! Now, there are many dry riverbeds and mere trickling streams.

It's dark, stars shining, the crescent moon has not yet risen, but Orion stands strong. Margaret, Nils and I are eating a meal of rice with dal and potatoes – and no chilies(!!!) and of course tea. At this point I must be physically addicted to tea – it's hot out so we must drink lots, and one must be sure that tea has been boiled – although we have no water purifying tablets – my halazone tablets are horrible as 5 tabs per quart are required, and then the water tastes like a swimming pool. But Margaret has some tablets from Switzerland that have no taste. We have two one-liter canteens – one we keep filled with tea! There are tea stops every half hour or so along the trails.

Today was a fairly easy trekking day although it was hot around noon. The sun is so very strong, and of course as we've only just begun our trek, we're not yet in shape. I have blisters all over my feet – and my $47 Fabiano trekking boots have a cracked-in-half sole – damn!

Somehow, no matter how hard I try to eliminate stuff, my pack is still full and pretty heavy. Clothes, soap, a little food: soy beans, candy bars, glucose powder. Margaret and Nils have rice, powdered milk… for lunch today we cooked rice and onions with cheese sauce – cheese which was very soft and going bad (it stunk!) from the heat, though it actually tasted really good! A few oranges – my diary and book, *Tibet* written by the Dalai Lama's brother.

The people here are very mellow; Buddhists. Prayer flags whipping in the wind, which is blowing fiercely. My sleeping bag shall feel great tonight – last night it was really warm just outside of Serencot. The people so far (up until here) have been obnoxious!

(Journal) Tuesday, April 8

Fierce dusty swirling winds drove us up the trail to Cherenkot, and finally the people around are "Ramro-tsa" – they're all so shitty in Serencot – still can't believe my sunglasses were stolen – and too many voices chanting "baksheesh."

Yes, it does get amazingly hot. I'm sweating so! And drinking so much! Was pleasant easy walking – downhill a little to Naudaunda – beautiful view of the mountains – wish we'd come earlier in March – so many clouds now, bummer. And my left boot has its sole cracked through to the leather – $47! Hope they last – blisters of course – sore from carrying my heavy pack also. Am considering staying in Bhiratante and saying the hell with Ghoripani – shall decide when the time comes – will spend at least two days there.

All day, all last night thinking of whether to go to Kashmir, or home from here – I've finally come to a pretty definite decision – although I wish to discuss all with David – almost two weeks since he left – seems so much longer – so many thoughts – so many friends.

I've decided to go to Delhi – via freak bus, hopefully – fly from Delhi to Amsterdam – then home. Who knows – maybe be with Margaret and Nils and hitch to Zurich. They have a plane to Amsterdam from Delhi on May 12 – spending 2 wk. in Amsterdam, then hitching home to Zurich.

It's 9:00 PM – time for sleeping.

(Journal) April 9

Such a wonderful day! Awoke to the sound of the roosters crowing – saw the sunrise, many intense clouds enshrouding the mountains – still so beautiful. We took our time getting started – only an hour and a half down – saw an Australian guy – he told me David was in Birathante – I flew down the trail – not only a waterfall, also Dave!

Beautiful town – a westerner showed me to the room where Dave was staying – told me he was at the waterfall. I found his pack, left mine next to it, and ran to the waterfall.

Aahhh! Reuniting – me running and slipping down the slope – to Dave's uplifted smiling face – and the most beautiful place I've ever been! Crystal clear water flowing down, forming a pool for swimming – so many rocks to sit upon – and dive from.

And friends – Margaret and Nils – Bob (Michigan), who's in the Peace Corps, and his girlfriend Patty, whose father is a big guy working with US Aid. We'll visit them in Kathmandu – been invited for lunch – looking forward to eating American food like tuna fish salad and pickles!

Birathante is gorgeous… I shall spend a few days here – maybe even come back on our way back to Pokhara.

It's so nice to be with Dave again! He looks well – strong – didn't even attempt the climb, as conditions were too severe. Left dopey Fred at the Annapurna Base Camp, as the Austrian doctor pulled out his hangnail and told him to stay off of his feet for 3 days.

(Journal) Thursday, April 10

Spent the whole day by the waterfalls – walked up and beyond the largest one to a place where we could see 3 at once, and the water was so deep and crystal clear. Reading *Black Elk Speaks* about the plight of the American Indians is oh so sad. Maybe there's something I'll be able to do to help…

(Journal) Friday, April 11

Bit of excitement last night: house caught on fire! It looked like it was spreading rapidly, so we packed everything up in record time, considering how much stuff we have – and took it to the other side of the bridge, along with Joanne from San Francisco (Bruce, her boyfriend, has Sahib's Knee). So – if it weren't for all the freaks organizing an assembly line for passing buckets of water – putting the fire out within 1/2 an hour. But the one house is pretty much finished and sadly 4 goats perished… There are so many freaks here in Birathani! Australians, Germans (Fred arrived from the sanctuary today). Seeing friends from Kathmandu – Garret from Boston, many familiar faces.

Another peaceful day by the waterfalls; washing me and some clothes – reading *Black Elk Speaks* – among the most incredibly moving books I've ever read – the plight of the American Indian – how sad it makes me – such an incredible people – so whole – one with the earth – the six grandfathers… bows and arrows, dancing, communicating with the heavens – and then, the white man – the ruthless US cavalry stealing all that belonged to them, including their freedom. I'd like sometime to spend time with Indians, to help in some small way, get to know some of those people.

(Journal) April 12

So nice to trek for only a short time! Awoke at 5:30, packed up, but didn't hit the road until almost 7:00. Many others on the road.

Never have I been in such a beautiful place – the water cascading down from the mountains – I can see it tumbling in between and around ageless rocks – serenity pervades my entire being as I sit here with friends. Not bothering to set up the tent – sleeping beneath the stars shall be great – perhaps the moon shall appear early tonight…

(Journal) April 13

Awoke reasonably early, broke camp and headed up the never-ending stone steps to Ulleri at around 8:00 AM. Took it really slow. Somehow I feel like a Nepali bus trying to gain momentum to climb, like the little engine that could…

Got to Ulleri around 10:30. As there are no villages between and we don't have any food, and it was only 12:00, there was no reason not to go on. At first the trail was tough – more stacks with the sun blaring down – goddamn Harigaly! I just wasn't enjoying myself at all – my left boot being cracked is becoming painful – the ball of my foot very tender and my right knee hurts… Yesterday on the way from Tikha Dunga down to our incredible campsite, I slipped and fell – all my weight on one knee (pack and all – pack weighs around 20-25 lb.), scraping it up a bit – one part is pretty deep. Anyway, soon after Ulleri, the trail entered a beautiful, dense forest filled with tree-sized rhododendrons in all colors although most have wilted now as they are past their peak. As we climbed higher, the trail was up and down, so cool and shaded! With streams and brooks and a few staircases and beautiful little teeny flowers, which of course I am saving.

Towards late afternoon blue sky appeared – raising our hopes of seeing the mountains. But David and I are camping in such a gorgeous field – the view of the mountains should be intense – they're so close by! Hopefully it'll be clear for a little while so we'll see them in the morning – at sunrise – saw Annapurna poking through a cloud – incredibly high – Bang is knocking us out now… (Bang is a "sleeping pill" made from marijuana.)

(Journal) April 14

Today is very cloudy and brisk! No mountains to see so we slept and slept rather than our plan to start the climb to Poon Hill. Here we are in a beautiful grassy field – ten minutes walk above Ghoripani – surrounded by rhododendrons in full bloom – pink, white, magenta, and on the pass, just above the field I can hear the sounds of a donkey caravan going by – they all wear large brass bells, which have such deep vibrating tones… and the beasts are decorated with plumes on their heads and brightly colored carpets or blankets…

It's good to have our tent – to be camping in such a peaceful place – awakening to the sounds of cows and buffaloes munching and monkeys scampering about, making lots of noise. Yesterday on the trail we saw lots of snow-apes – all very white and hairy with black faces! Some are really large!

Today Grandpa would've been 84 years old; I pray that wherever he is, there is peace. And all my love goes home to Grammy, Mommy and Dad, who I know are now sending their love to me.

(Journal) April 15

Sitting around a beautiful warming fire with friends – today we're heading over Dearali pass to Gandrang – decided against going to Tato Pani, as it would take an extra 3 or 4 days. My visa runs out April 21. Actually, although it's more beautiful here than anywhere I've ever been, I'm anxious to get back to Kathmandu and find out what's up, whether or not the $350 has been sent. I hope so!

Today we caught glimpses of the mountains; Annapurna rising above all – amazing. Now the wind is blowing fiercely – there's the feeling of spring in the air…

Mike, Tony, Matt (all from Australia), Vernon, Garret, and Dave and I will trek together. We'll take 2 days to Gandrang, sleeping in the shelter on the pass, about 4 hours' walk from here.

(Journal) Wednesday, April 16, 1975

I can't believe that today is my birthday and I am nineteen years old and in one of the most beautiful places I've ever been. By a flowing river, steep hillsides all around, with rhododendrons in full bloom… Yesterday was a perfect trekking day except for an attack of the shits… Mostly downhill – not steep at all – through incredibly colorful forests – rhododendrons of all colors: bright x-mas red, pink, magenta, white – even purple! And all sorts of other smelling nice flowers – found many for this book.

Arrived at the hut at around 3:30 PM. Got a fire together for some tea – then cooked up some soup. And then we all mandraxed out (Mandrax is a strong sleeping pill that was outlawed in the U.S. years ago, but is purchased over the counter in this part of the world). We played a very messed up card game of "I doubt it" – … I was so high!!!

Can't say I've ever been in a more beautiful place on my birthday – the trekking was easy – gentle – down, down for a while, then up – but not bad when you take it slow… and through the most gorgeous forest. And eagles and hawks gliding high above… representing freedom.

As we walked along, there was a steep hillside directly to our left obscuring views of anything beyond. Suddenly the hillside dropped off, and I decided to walk up a few yards from the trail, and suddenly there was Macchapachure, the fishtail, rising in all its glory – and the Annapurnas – so fierce and proud. Of course we stopped for a break – biscuits and my last sappy bar.

I do hope I'll meet up again with some of the friends I've met… paths will inevitably cross again.

Well – it looks like we'll be heading home soon – me anyway – so many unanswered questions – who will be there – and will there be false relationships built up – old friends and even family trying to mold me back into the position I played before I left? And I'll be doing the same thing – but I'm sure I've changed a helluva lot, as have my friends. It will be difficult to adjust. It will take lots of time – it's difficult to know – and speculating only makes me more unsure… guess I'll just have to wait and see! It won't be long!

Tomorrow, we'll be heading back to Birathanti and the beautiful waterfalls!

(Journal) April 17

Not a bad walk down from Gandrung although it certainly was warm out. Dave woke everyone up this morning to see the most beautiful sunrise. Crystal clear sky with the Annapurnas and Machapachure so tremendous and white. It was totally overwhelmingly beautiful. Most of the way down today, the mountains remained in view.

Now we're back in Birathanti feeling refreshed after swimming and washing beneath the first waterfall. And finally I had my can of fruit cocktail – mmm!

We're staying in the first house after the bridge and the people are so nice, not so paisa-conscious as they are around the corner. And I think we're the only westerners. We've got our own private balcony with a great view of Macchapacchure…

(Journal) April 19

Yesterday we spent all day by the 2nd waterfall. Dean – who's from Wisconsin and has been traveling four years now – been working in Munich for a while – Dave and he remember meeting somewhere in the East 2 years ago. And Garret – we cooked up some onions and potatoes – Nepali cooking oil is really raunchy! So – poor Garret found a huge tick in his right elbow – got it out no problem – but a pain is shooting up his arm so he's heading straight back for a blood test.

We packed up and started up here to Chandracot at around 5:30. It's so pleasant to be able to take my time and climb! Arrived around 7:00 – never once running out of breath. Again stayed at "The Best" hotel, but somehow it wasn't so good – or rather, the lady was really a cheapskate.

(Journal) Sunday, April 20 - The Grande Finale

Yes, 'twas a very long day from Chandracot to Pokhara, but we made it! Don't know what it is about my luck – felt a twinge in the back of my right knee – maybe a pulled tendon. Yesterday there was a big festival, and all along the trail we saw Nepalis all dressed up – the women in red and/or pink – so many buffaloes, goats, and sheep being led to slaughter, and strange music processions – long (5 or 6 foot) brass horns, and drums – then a little boy from Serencot recognized me and told me that my sunglasses were at the "hotel" in Serencot – others confirmed this. So the 14-year-old boy accompanied us and I actually got them back!

Feeling absolutely exhausted, we began the downward trek to Pokhara, Phewatal urging us on. As usual, we lost our way – there are so many blasted trails! Stumbling down – halfway it began to rain – goddammit! Luckily Garret had just given us a poncho, so we each had one to put over us. Just as we got down to the rice paddies, it began to hail, like mothballs pelting downwards!

I guess that yesterday's festival was for rain – and it certainly rained! Ten minutes before the hail really began, we arrived, soaking wet, at the house I stayed at before. The English couple, Neil and Wendy, still are living upstairs, and Vicki from Michigan is living in both downstairs rooms, but she let us sleep in her "living room." She's really nice; I feel close to her. And this morning we moved to a double room in the Lake View Hotel.

It really was a beautiful trek. Never have I seen anything so beautiful as the rhododendron forests between Ghoripani and Gandrung. And once we got away from Pokhara Valley, the people became mellower…

And now, back in Pokhara – as usual, nothing changes and reunions are always happening. Here at the Bhatterhai is Gary from Toronto whom we knew in Goa. He's planning to find a house and mellow out here for a while – doesn't everyone want to stay here?

(Journal) April 21

So we booked the minibus for Thursday. We've moved to a little house near Krishna's house – haven't even seen it yet – while I was at the airport David moved us in.

Saw Vicki and Sammie this morning, buying veggies at the airport. They're both 24 – both spent a while working in Australia. Sammie worked with juvenile delinquents, aged 13-17. That would be very interesting – I'm thinking maybe when I get home, I'll try something like that – it's not fair for me to say that I'm sure I want to work with retarded children because that's the only thing I've tried – time to broaden my scope.

Lately I've been thinking that maybe somewhere like "Friend's World" would be good for me – that if I did go to a structured "college" with a classroom scene – it would be a sort of cop-out, having things laid out for me – even though it'd be really difficult to get into studying – it would be good to have to use my mind and set up my own lifestyle – maybe take a course in meditation – work with kids – research – I just don't know yet…

(Journal) Tuesday, April 22

We spent a nice day by the river near the Tibetan camp. The monsoons are here to stay – it's rained for 3 days in a row now – but I don't think it's raining in Kathmandu – hope not! Apparently, Pokhara valley gets 150 inches of rain per year!

Our last day in Pokhara! This little adobe house we've stayed in for the past couple of nights is really nice. There are 3 adjoining rooms; a French couple sleeps in one, their kitchen is in the middle and we're on the end. Outside there's the nicest toilet in Pokhara – bamboo square "room" – all a bamboo floor.

How I'll miss this place – this incredible valley – I can see those white peaks rising above all – spreading their peace throughout all beings…

This time our good-byes will be for a much longer time – who knows when I'll be back… Good-byes are oh so difficult for me!

Had a beautiful talk with Sammie, today – she's so kind and understanding – so perceptive to others' feelings. It feels good to talk with someone who's in pretty much the same head as myself – she told me how it was working with the kids in Australia, that one really learns a lot about oneself – especially working with older kids who are capable of hurting your feelings, or playing mind games – many times it would be difficult to cope with.

Oh, there are so many things to get into – so many people who need help: blacks all over the states, American Indians, underprivileged ghetto children, 3rd world countries. I literally have the whole world in my hands – guess the best way is to take it as it comes.

I'll miss Vicki and Sammie – two really beautiful ladies – again, friendships begin to blossom and must be cut short – 'tis inevitable… perhaps paths shall cross again sometime!

Pokhara really is truly the most gorgeous place I've ever been, and tonight is so very clear – with the moon only 4 or so days away from being full – and the mountains are in absolute stupendous snowy view! Never in all the time we've been here have they showed themselves so magnificently at night! And there's so much snow now that it's pre-monsoon – every day it's crystal clear from sunrise until around 8 or 9 – then the clouds begin to obscure the mountains – then they gradually come closer and closer, and cover the valley til it's about 2:30 – then there's no sunlight – it becomes quite cool, and amazing thunder and lightning begin to happen; sounds like a war! And the skies really do open up, but around sunset, it begins to clear – amazing views are again offered!

I'll miss this beautiful valley! Don't know when, but I do know I'll be back some day!!!

Sun rising over the mountains was so special on my last morning – crystal clear – the mountains seeming to grow as more snow falls upon them. Yes I'm sad to leave, but "all things must pass… and others will soon fill the voids."

Back in Kathmandu… it's so busy and crowded after mellowing out for so many days and suddenly having to do things and think about future plans… ahhh!

And everyone at home is expecting me soon – how I miss them all – I still am definitely planning to be home in June sometime – who knows what the hell will be happening when I get there – at least I know there'll be tons of love!

And who did we see in "Himalayan cold Drinks?!" Ulla and Ressu… they ran out of money and returned early from the Everest trek. So good reuniting with friends. Bob's not at the Pleasure Lodge any longer – I hear he's out living with Tibetans somewhere in Kathmandu Valley. And Terry's still here – saw Steve… Terry's becoming more and more spaced out – is almost out of touch – makes me so sad.

(Journal) April 26

Sitting in "The Don't Pass Me By" together we all headed for the Chai and Pie – then on to the Match Box – (w/out Robin and Sayward) heard there would be a party happening. On the way we saw strange musical marching processions – and by the Bagmati River a body was burning upon a wood fire – people moaning and praying – so happy – then at The Matchbox there was a French woman who made us coffee in her room – sat around playing music – only a few people.

On the way "home" we heard and saw a large uniformed marching band – typical Hindu wedding – always such incredible pageantry! Kathmandu really is magical under a full moon and beautiful. Because it was Friday night, all the pagodas and temples were lit up, ahhhh, like a dream!

(Journal) April 27

Spent a much needed day of rest in "Little America" yesterday. Swimming, Ping-Pong, tuna, lettuce, and mayonnaise sandwich – Fanta root beer… all Americans. I met Peace Corps workers, and one of the Israeli embassy guys, Zohar, who says there are only 3 of them! I must admit that I'm getting more and more homesick – missing my family so very much. Soon enough, soon enough! We've been invited to Patty's house for dinner on Tuesday night – I do wish Bob would be there, but he's gone back to his village – won't be seeing him until the states.

Now, sitting in "The United" with Terry and a couple whom we met at Benanli – up the beach a ways from Colva. Didn't do much all day – washed, cleaned the room up (finally!). Bruce and Joanne came up for a while – really good people – friends – Bruce is 32, Joanne is 28 – big deal, what does age mean anyway?

Playing Hatikva under a golden moon and the big dipper straight above, and looking out toward Swayambhunath knowing some of its mysteries.

Received a registered letter back from Roy – our film reached home! Yeah! Roy finds it so strange – "spacey" to be home. Eli designed such an incredible mandala – so heavy – he had it embroidered (machine… chain stitch). Dave took a picture of it.

(Journal) Wednesday, April 30

Met John and Tim by the "Yin Yang" and together we took a taxi out to Patty's house, not far from Shanta Bhagwan in a beautiful neighborhood, other diplomats. UN people, etc. lived all around. But no house could be in a nicer place – never have I seen such an incredible view of Kathmandu Valley! The house itself is gorgeous – very modern brick – could be found anywhere on Belmont Hill. And beautifully decorated inside (of course the lawns are perfect, also), so tastefully done. If only Mom could see it! Such incredible pieces of art the Murthas have collected from all the places they have lived – statues, carpets, Rajasthani pillow covers, wall hangings, artifacts of different kinds. And they have five servants – and a great dog named Kelly – the biggest teddy-bear black poodle I've ever seen…

But as good a time as I had, I became so homesick, especially when Patty's parents came home from a cocktail party. I sat talking with Mrs. Murtha who's a really nice lady – couldn't help from crying – reminded me of Mom. Oh, I wish I were on my way home now.

Meanwhile, I mentioned that Mr. Murtha was head of US Aid for Nepal. His previous post had been Saigon. While we were feasting on the much awaited tuna salad, Lays potato chips, and Fanta Orange soda, they'd gone to a cocktail party at the home of the US Ambassador's. Less than an hour after they left they returned home, and Mr. Murtha's face was ashen. That was the night the US pulled out of Saigon officially ending the Vietnam War. Mr. Murtha asked us to leave so he could focus on "getting his people out" before all hell would break loose.

I remember how odd it felt to find out the war was over while America still slept, as we were nine time zones ahead.

CHAPTER FIFTEEN

IT'S HARD TO SAY GOODBYES

KATHMANDU

(Journal) May 2

Sitting in the Hungry Eye with Bob and Kali (we reunited at the Mandala) and headed to our "penthouse." A bunch of people came up. One guy had a guitar so he and Dave played. My damn tooth was hurting so – don't know what I'm going to do. Sure couldn't play my flute!

Today we'll check Nepal Rastra Bank. And a decision must be reached. Shall we go to Kashmir? Joanne wants for me to fly to Lukla with her because Bruce's knee is still bad. It sounds tempting… who knows when I'll get back home – but already it's May, and Vicki and Ellen are in Kashmir… but will we find a ride there? Do we have enough money to fly? Or should we just forget about it and head for Europe…

(Journal) May 3 - Ganga Lodge

Last night we cooked a delicious meal with Margaret and Nils consisting of fried veggies, then a stew with zucchini, tomatoes, onions, carrots, string beans, and cheese! Dave picked up some masala, which very closely resembles oregano. Anyway, halfway through the meal it began to rain followed by intense lightning like the night we were on our way home from

Amherst and Guru Maharaj's festival, and strangely enough, the Guru was in town today! So the rain came pouring down and into our room in about 10 different places… such idiots running the Mt. Everest! We stayed there the night and found this nice huge room – 4 beds just for us – one whole wall is all windows – with screens! And Ulla and Ressu live here, and Jeff (NY) and Howard and Fran from Boston – they got married at Swayambhu – a Tibetan Buddhist wedding – witnessed by the American consul (a real jerk apparently) – legally registered and all. And Ulla and Ressu are considering getting married. I will miss them immensely.

Lately I've been depressed. We're stuck here waiting for money, not knowing whether or not it's coming. My tooth must be pulled – sitting in the dentist's office – a Nepali with a degree from Osaka University. First he removed the silver from my lower right 12-year molar – all black and oozing beneath – really sickening. It seems so useless that I must lose a tooth. Dad and Mom will be so angry.

The whole scene around here is depressing. There are so many freaks – I'm tired of them – although I do have good friends. Ulla and Ressu, Margaret and Nils (who've gone to Bhadgaon for a few days), Joanne and Bruce, Julie and Nina, Terry (finally he received his money!), Bob – who's now living out at Bhodanath. Yes, I consider these people my friends – but good-byes must be said to all – it's inevitable. I wish to go home, to gather friends about me there.

Last night the reality of David and me struck… we both know there is an end not so very far away. Oh how it shall hurt both of us equally I think. Yes, everything everyone at home told me is true and though I knew it all along, I was/am unable to live for tomorrow. I wonder if ever this shall change?

I am oh so weary of the East – of the filth and inefficiency. Yes, it's inexpensive to live here, but paid for by added frustrations. I miss people at home so much, yet I can be certain only of my family being there for me; I am very lucky. They are incredible people, and their strength and love shall help to guide me along the path I choose.

Dave's gone to Swayambhu with Bruce and Joanne. It's peaceful here at the Ganga Lodge. This large sun-filled room is a pleasure to sit in; I'm almost finished reading *Tibet* – a really beautiful book, so much to teach. The birds are incredible and I'm glad to be away from Freak Street. I feel myself loosening up already!

Yesterday's fight with the fat hotel manager from the Mt. Everest Lodge was a royal bummer. I just can't believe (or tolerate) the stupidity of some people, as if that rain were the first ever in Kathmandu. We tried to not pay for our bill, saying film was ruined by water, but we had no evidence. At least we could've got a little discount for the inconvenience – hah! Instead we had to get the police – damn, it was such an Indian scene – Nepalis pouring out of the very cracks in the walls…

Reading *Summerhill* I think of Ned Ryerson with gratitude. He's so full of wisdom and so gentle. So thrilled he created Palfrey and I had the privilege of attending for that one life-changing year! Wondering how he is – and my other friends from Palfrey St. School. Caroline – I'm sad to be drifting away – perhaps someday paths shall meet again…

(Journal) Today is the birth date of Buddha - May 5

Somehow I haven't felt very inspired to write – guess it's because nothing new has been happening. Today we went to the consulate and they are sending a telex to Cedric and we should receive a reply by Thursday – we hope! Getting tired of hanging out in Kathmandu although there certainly couldn't be any nicer city to be stuck in! Somehow, though, we haven't gotten it together to get out of here even for a day! And the double decker bus we saw in Istanbul is here preparing to take riders back to Europe. There's a slight possibility we'll be on it… depending on our money situation!

A man sits every day on the same corner; his lips moving in silent prayer. For hours he just sits, hands cupped upon his lap, maybe a few paisa in his palm. He looks through unseeing eyes – beseeching my inner soul with the thought that I am so very lucky. Who am I not to give? I have so very much! But alas, it is not possible for me to give to all… and I frown upon myself for becoming as hardened as I am – not so much toward this sightless man, or the sick woman nearby. One day I walked by – it was oh so saddening. I turned around and gave her a rupee making her

But in the future, the very near future, emotional attachments won't have to end abruptly as I settle myself down and begin to get into people, helping them.

I'm finding it very difficult to focus upon what I'll do when I get home because then, for the first time in my life I shall be forced to make my own decisions. I've got the whole world in my hands – I guess I'll just have to take things as they come (What else is new?!).

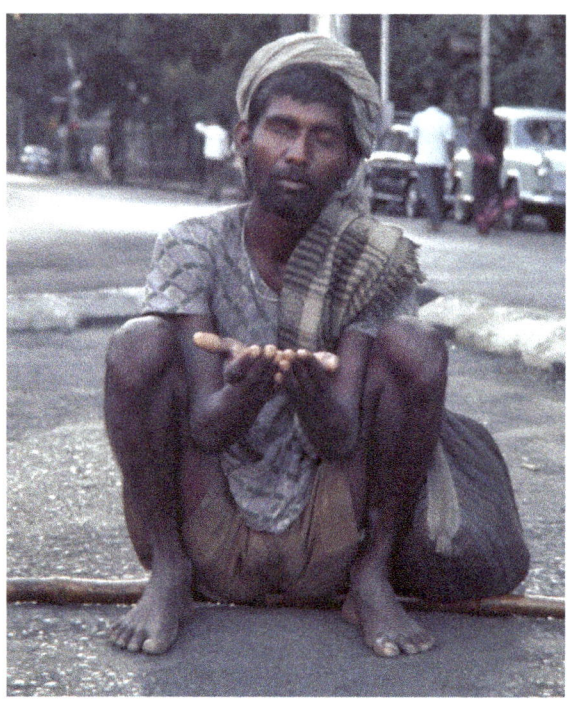

whole day brighter. That rupee meant so much to her! And all day every day we spend rupees like pennies…

It brought tears to my eyes and even to David's! But the children around always touching me, pulling on my arm and putting on sad faces, "Meemee… chea khani." I now react almost violently and push them away, which I'm not proud of. I guess it's because I wish I could give to all – especially love to homeless little ones. But I don't want to give, as the emotional attachments only hurt as they must come to an inevitable end.

And today I read all of May 5's *Time Magazine* – it's hard to believe the war in Vietnam is actually over, that the communists have taken over South Vietnam. Very powerful to have been at the home of the Murtha's, head of US AID for Nepal and formerly of Saigon, the night the US pulled out of Saigon. What a trip.

(Journal) Thursday, May 8

Well, still no word from anyone at home – hopefully tomorrow there'll be a reply telex at the consul. We spent the afternoon by the pool with Patty and were practically the only people there. Weekdays are like that. Every day is hotter than the one before so we feel lucky to be able to escape to the pool. The city gets to be a drag.

I just remembered something amazing that happened while Dave and I sat outside of the tent at Ghoripani. There was a satellite! At first I thought it was a shooting star, but it kept going – beginning at one side of the sky, quickly moving between stars and planets toward infinity – incredibly fast…

(Journal) Sunday, May 11

Still in Kathmandu wanting to get out, still no word from anyone – not even an answering telex! So frustrating! I guess if we hear nothing by tomorrow then I'll have to call home. I hate to do that! It will frighten Mom and Dad, and I know I'll probably get so emotional that all I'll be able to do is cry, that is, if we can even get a connection!

So, lately many friends have left: Ulla and Ressu, and Julie and Nino all went on the double decker – 46 people to Delhi! And yesterday, Angie and Ashok flew to Delhi and then on to London. I gave Angie a birthday card for Deb, a letter for Sue, and Dave wrote one to Cedric, which Angie'll post from London on Monday. Margaret and Nils are flying to Benares on Wednesday. Their flight from Delhi to Amsterdam leaves on the 19th – can't believe that May is half over! Wish we were joining them…

Last night we ate dinner at A.K. Sherpa's house. He's got a really nice cement house on the main road, 5 minutes before Boudhnath. His wife is very beautiful, but we hardly saw her for more than 10 minutes as she doesn't speak English, plus A.K.'s attitude toward women is just like all other Easterners which makes me so angry! They have four incredibly beautiful children (with a fifth on the way). Three girls, ages 8, 5, and 18 months, and a crazy little boy, almost 4. The girls sang the English songs they've learned in school: "Mary had a Little Lamb," "Skip to my Lou," "Twinkle, Twinkle," etc. They sounded so cute with their accents. I couldn't believe it when they sang "One Little, Two Little, Three Little Nepalis," cracked me up!

(Journal) Wednesday, May 14

There's so much to write! On Monday morning, the $350 finally arrived at the Embassy, sent by Roy. So now that the money has arrived we can begin to move – buy a few things and split.

Just an hour ago we wished Margaret and Nils farewell as their taxi headed down New Road to the airport. They're flying to Benares where they will stay for one day, and then take the train to Delhi. On May 19, they will fly to Amsterdam! I'm so glad we'll see them in Zurich… that is if Mom sends me $200. Damn! I really do want to buy some things – during the whole trip I've been putting it off – and now we don't have any money…

Last night we ate at the Indira – the best food I've had in quite a while – expensive for here, but very cheap by western standards. Dave, me, Nils, Margaret, and Joanne – Bruce wasn't feeling well. And Steve is really sick – has amoebic dysentery, plus a respiratory disease. Bummer! But at least he didn't get sick on the trek.

As anxious as I am to get home – to get to the West – it will be so difficult to say goodbye to Kathmandu and to all my friends here… We've been traveling for almost 8 months now, and 4 out of those 8 months have been spent in Nepal. In a sense I really feel at home here. I'm able to do as I please, go where I want, when I want with no pressures. No heavy decisions to be made – yes, it's been an amazing vacation! But now, it's drawing to a close and I have such mixed feelings!

All is so tranquil here – one is free to be as she/he chooses. Any time of day or night it is safe to walk alone… and in a month or so I'll actually be home in Belmont! It's simply too bewildering to even think about because there's just no way I can possibly know what it'll be like until I get there. Except I know the whole western standard of living will hit me like a cyclone – fixed prices for everything! What a drag – and high prices. And no street vendors except at Red Sox games or something. Unlike Asia, one just doesn't see life outside on the streets – only people walking on streets, sidewalks, ducking into stores, offices.

Oh, how I shall miss the Nepalis! The ladies sitting on street corners, selling peanuts – 1.40 rupees per manna… or oranges 2 for a rupee… or assorted cigarettes and mithi (sweets)… some even have Salems for just 50 paisa each. And this is the season for the funny red berries with the pits – or the orange ones looking just like raspberries and tasting so sweet.

And on the street where "Ma's Fountain of Youth" restaurant was (before it burned down four days ago) at the intersection with New Road there's a "people tree". It's a tremendous banyan tree surrounded by fruit vendors selling delicious mangoes, newspapers, shoeshine boys, and there's a movie theater down the street, where we saw a great Russian (Pushkin) fairy tale dubbed in English. It was quite impressive! The Russians sure know how to make pictures! The feature was preceded by a film of the king's coronation. Wish we could have been here – such pageantry!

And New Road, the perfect name, with all its tourist shops and imported novelties bullshit which the Nepalis dig so much… And there's the amazingly old, tremendous Brahma bull that hangs out… and the park in front of Nepal Bank Ltd. And the Indira restaurant with beggars out front. We've found that there really aren't very many beggars here in Kathmandu – just the orphaned children I've mentioned before. They are especially present on Freak Street where all us Western travelers hang out. Again, I have mixed feelings. I feel sorry for these children, that they actually do live on the streets as in winter they really are cold. Some of them are sweet… Yet after a while their demanding ways become obnoxious. I don't know, maybe they really are hungry!

I don't know his name, but one 8 yr. old boy, such a little beauty! Anyway, in November and December he used to always come to me, cling to me, telling me he had no parents (which I found out was the truth). My heart strings were definitely tweaked… I used to buy him food. But I found myself really beginning to care – something I'm just not able to afford, mentally or financially at this stage of my life.

This boy speaks English very well and seems far more intelligent than the average Nepali. One day, while sitting at the Bhatterhai Restaurant in Pokhara, I saw the same boy, sparkling clean, wearing shiny new shoes, and a new western outfit – pants, shirt, how white his teeth are! A French monk and his friend recognized the child as something special, and took him under their wing, tried to get him into a monastery in Pokhara, but the monasteries in the valley are very poor, and already two orphans were living there. When we came back in March, the same boy was back on "Freak Street" – same clothes, quite a bit dirtier and worn… He told me he's living in a temple – don't know if any food is provided for him – regardless, he was right back into it – except now, because he's not dressed in rags, he's entitled to enter restaurants and make straight for soft hearts like mine. But having the western clothing is also to his disadvantage outside, because tourists are more inclined to give to worse-off looking children. I'm happy to say that none of them look too dreadful as there are plenty of other travelers who give to them as I do.

Now, the boy is working in the United Restaurant. Last night he had the nerve to ask (whispered in my ear), "one rupee baksheesh, Mimi" – I told him sternly that there was no way I'd baksheesh him – what about his friends outside, cold and hungry…

Freak Street… there's just no place in the world like it – Handicraft shops, provisional stores carrying eggs, bread, shampoo, sweets, munchies, hotels and lodges…"Monument Lodge," "Oriental," "Century," "Pleasure Lodge," "Annapurna Lodge," "Mt. Everest Lodge," with its fat turd manager – and the ever white cleaners just beyond – 2 rupees to wash my cruddy, filthy jeans, and restaurants: "The Little Mandarin," "Eat at Joe's," "The Earth," "The United," "Snowman Cold Drinks" (mmm – nothing like a mixed fruit with cashew nut lassi…), "The Don't Pass Me By," "The Old Hungry Eye," "The Yellow Star" (yecchhh!), "Modern Pie," etc…

And trading stores – eager for western goods such as jeans, boots, jackets. Packing agencies, travel agents; today we bought our plane tickets from Kathmandu to Delhi from Natraj Tours and Travels.

I can't believe we're splitting so soon!

And as you make your way slowly up the street, amidst bicycles (many for rent at only 3 Rp. a day – 1 rupee for an hour – a great deal – not bad bikes, either!), rickshaws, careening crazy taxi drivers… and so many freaks! Now all the French junkies are here having been chased away from Goa by the heat. They really are a yucky-looking bunch… mostly very freaky-looking, always spaced, henna hair all matted, wearing sarongs – barefoot, some with tracks on their arms from shooting up heroin.

Met a French guy yesterday who we remember meeting at the Peace Hotel in Kandahar. A bunch of us sat around on that beautiful grassy yard smoking joints. I remember he came out with the largest water pipe I've ever seen – I guess it was actually a hookah, made of porcelain, standing three feet off the ground. The bowl was about 8 inches in diameter filled with big chunks of hashish with the Government of Afghanistan stamp of approval embossed on it. Keeping the hash lit were pieces of burning charcoal… What a trip! About six people including us were there. Each person took about 6 hits at once and collapsed on the floor choking. When it was passed to me, I could hardly even inhale a little. It turned out that that French guy was busted at the Pakistani border and spent 31 days in an Afghani prison. He said he really dug it there, as he got high all the time with the Afghani prisoners and guards!

The black market's been good lately! 13.50 for cash and at the Panorama Hotel we got 12.15 for travelers' cheques! And as one make one's way up Freak Street, or to use its real name, Jochhen Tole, so many hot-shot Nepalis come up, saying, "Change money? You want hashish? Ganga? You want to buy, to sell, to trade…" Certainly gets a bit annoying after a while – but it's all part of the scene which I'll miss! And I'd be remiss if I didn't mention the construction worker at the end of the street by Durbar Square who wears a Pink Floyd Dark Side of the Moon T-shirt on most days.

So many familiar faces: the shopkeepers, restaurant employees, Ton and Raju, and of course Jim who finally got his money! And on

Friday, he shall fly to Bangkok and then home to California. He's been in India and Nepal only since April 1973!!! Good luck to Jim.

Friends, friends, friends: Joanne and Bruce, Cathy, Steve, and Frank, Patty, Martha – tonight I called her – her dad is being transferred to head up US AID in Colombia in three weeks. Must be quite an interesting life living in foreign countries as a diplomat representing the USA. We'll meet Patty on Friday night in front of the Yin and Yang and we'll go to Peter's place together.

Delhi on Monday?? Can't say I'm looking forward to being there. Oh, the heat will be incredible. I can't even imagine! It's pre-monsoon and well over 100 degrees… close to 120, I hear! I do hope we can afford an air-conditioned hotel! And that we'll find ourselves a quick flight to Amsterdam…

There are so many beautiful things I'd love to buy for myself and as gifts. In 8 months on the road I've hardly bought anything. Whenever I'd want something Dave would suggest that I wait. Or I would figure I'd find something nicer, or that I didn't want to schlep things around for months… Yet now that it's come time to head homeward, we're running very low on funds – and I can't afford much – goddamn it! I'd love to find a nice rug for Mom – and an old prayer wheel, or Tibetan cymbals for Uncle Neuman (they gave me $50 asking if I might find them something cool!). Perhaps I'll find something out at Boudhnath. Also, I really should find something for Grammy and for Auntie Eleanor and Daddy! I have pouches and pretty boxes for my friends.

I'll even miss Nepali matches that either break or refuse to light! And lizards so amazingly fast…

And The Pie Shops – The New Style has reopened – mmm! Apricot pie, banana cake, coffee cake, apple-date cake, fudgy brownies – and Pig Street really is a classic… Where else in the world are there a bunch of fantastic pie shops on a street next to a murky, muddy (pre-monsoon) river with several gigantic pigs lolling in the mud…

And then there's our beloved Swayambhu where we've spent so many amazing days and nights over the four months we've been here. On our last night here we should go to Swayambhu and on up those stairs to the stupa. Too bad the full moon is still a ways away. Tonight was the new moon with a few clouds drifting along, in no way obscuring the stars.

Oh, Kathmandu, beautiful valley with mellow people – oblivious to the world outside – easy going, free to wander as you like. May the western world never completely wrap you up. The mountains shall always remain unconquered – no matter how many people climb to the tops. They are just so vast – solid, spreading peace…

(Journal) Thursday, May 15

Today Debbie turned 17 and Daddy 47. Damn… time really has flown by! We only have three more full days here, which makes me sad. Today we went out to Patan by taxi with Joanne and Bruce. There is a Tibetan refugee camp where the Tibetans spin wool and weave gorgeous rugs. Found a rug for Mom, but didn't buy it yet – tomorrow I shall – 325 Rp.

Midnight

Good-bye to Jim – he now walks down the driveway, heading through the quiet night-time streets of Kathmandu one last time to Harry's Lodge. Of course he cruised on up to Swayambhu where we also will go on Sunday night – our last night! I just can't believe it – Delhi on Monday and hopefully Amsterdam before the weekend!

And now Jerry and Mike stay next door. They play guitar and sing, which is nice. They met in Israel on a kibbutz in the Jordan Valley and will be returning to Israel shortly. I'm a bit envious. Wonder how my Israeli friends are?

From Patan we took a 15 rupee taxi to Boudha to shop. I was so pissed off by the prices! All so ridiculously high with very little bargaining due to all the dumb tourists. Throughout our time in Asia we've considered ourselves travelers rather than tourists. I bought a pale pink silk Tibetan blouse (for wearing with my Tibetan dress). Managed to get the shopkeeper down from 40 to 30. I also bought a small silver and turquoise bead; the green in the turquoise matches my choker (which still sits in my pocket, as leather is so difficult to find). The piece is being made into a ring for my small finger.

(Journal) May 16

It's almost 1:00 AM – May 17 actually. We just returned from "Peter's Place" – haven't been to a discotech for a long time! Had a good time. I miss dancing! Not live music, but good;

Stevie Wonder, The Stones. Patty was there, and Zohar with his girlfriend who is one of the 14 girls here studying for a semester. Zohar is dynamite; wish I'd gotten to know him better! Very crowded – mostly by Nepali guys. We met some of Patty's friends and got really good feelings from them.

This morning I went out to Patan again with Joanne and Bruce – bought the 2 foot X 3 foot carpet for 320 rupees. It really is beautiful and I hope Mom likes it! If not, I sure do! Only two more days here…

And today, Dave received a telegram from Jerry, saying that he sent $100 to Delhi for us! So I guess we'll definitely be going to Paris! He really is amazing – but also, a letter from Gary arrived – things aren't going so well on that end – Dave's mom is in a hospital – poor woman is so messed up – and all rests on Davey's shoulders when he gets home as he's the oldest and the most together. He'll have to be out looking for a job immediately. It's too much responsibility for anyone aged 21 – he should be free to lead his own life rather than have to take care of his parents.

Finally the time has come to say goodbye to Kathmandu. I am so sad to leave! How I'll miss the smiling Nepali faces greeting me with "Namasté," and the freeness of this place where I can feel comfortable wherever I want doing anything – no hassles with people… only the hustlers on Freak "ees" Street… "change money, you want buy hashish? You have something for selling, trading…?" Yes, I'll even miss them.

Especially, it's so hard to say good-bye to friends – good friends like Cathy, Steve, and Frank. Cathy promises to visit us at home as they make their way from Montreal to their hometown of Savannah, Georgia in a few months. We had a delicious good-bye meal at the Utse, and are now sitting in the "New Style Pie" shop – mmm… that chocolate cream really makes it!

CHAPTER SIXTEEN

A GRAND FINALE AT A FIVE STAR HOTEL!

DELHI

(Journal) May 17

Today has been a trip – the flight more spectacular than any I've ever taken before, up above the clouds with the high Himalaya rising through them – Maccapachure, the Annapurnas, Dhaulighiri… Never has that mountain impressed me so! I hadn't realized how massive it is, got lots of good shots.

As we landed in Delhi the stewardess announced that it was 100° out – a small relief as I'd heard it was 115°. Very hot, but not nearly as bad as I'd expected. Customs, both Indian and Nepali, were a breeze and my pack was barely looked at.

And now we're sitting in the courtyard of Mrs. Mowyah's Guest House in New Delhi, just around the corner from the Quality Restaurant on Parliament Street, also just around the corner from the Mohan Singh Building. We heard about this place from Mark (print shop guy in Kathmandu). We took a taxi along with John and Ruthie from British Columbia. They are around 30. He's a pharmacist and she's a teacher. I really like them.

We headed straight to the American Express office where I happily received 2 letters from Mom and one from Jeri, an absolute classic! Can't wait to see her as she's probably grown so much. I imagine I'll have to get to know her as she's probably changed a lot. I imagine I must have changed a lot and that reuniting with my family and friends will seem both normal and strange at the same time.

Now that we're in Delhi, that we finally said good-bye to Kathmandu, the reality of going home is beginning to freak me out; it's so close – just don't know what it'll be like. One thing for sure: I'm beginning a whole new life! Also, a letter from Archana who cares so much for me, and is so sincere, so innocent, so beautiful. The way she professes her love for me is a bit much. I guess it's because Indian women have no real social life. Never a boyfriend, they meet their husbands only a short time before the marriage. It sure seems ridiculous to me!

And our Hindi teacher TC wrote! Didn't realize how much he's thought of us.

We should've written to him long ago. He's such a lonely soul, holed up in his stuffy 3rd floor room studying Sanskrit, getting his PhD in it at Harvard.

Mom keeps me well informed about family and friends. She called Agnes who said that Dave's mom is in Waltham State Hospital needing shock treatments. Oh, it makes me so sad especially to be aware of the shit David must face when he gets home. He really is one of the strongest people I know. I respect him lots for this – don't know what'll happen with us... I do know I need to spend some time alone...

We were lucky that today was cooler than it's been lately. I wouldn't mind going on Wednesday, but Delhi is a food trip! A trip of all sorts – but I overdid it on the fruit – a fruit salad with ice cream, mango, papaya, pineapple, apricot, apples, oranges – then to "The Milk Bar" – a slice of an ice cream cake – vanilla, pistachio, strawberry, pineapple with nuts – then a bottle of pineapple milk – lots of water and a huge glass of sugarcane juice with lime – was (am still) so full I couldn't eat dinner.

People to meet everywhere, into so many far-out trips like this guy we met from Quebec. He has been in India for 5 years. He has money, a jeep, incredible old tankas, Chinese carpet – wish I had more money...

It's going to be heavy culture shock flying into Paris from here – from one extreme to the other – yet both are so vast and bustling. Ruthie was telling me places to visit, like Le Louvre. But unless I plan to spend a few days there and wander around, it's best to plan out what I'd like to see. Also, she said I "have to" walk down the street next to the Champs Elysees – the highest of fashion where everyone dresses to kill and all the famous designers have their shops along with the top cosmetics lines. It'll be so strange to be in a world of fashion after wearing the same hiking clothes for so long. I'm sure it'll be very interesting, but overpowering, and I'll feel like such a slob... I do wish we were going to Amsterdam to ease the transition from East to West; there I know the feeling must be warm as there are lots of freaks. Now it's time to psych myself up for Paris.

As hard as I try, it's impossible to write up all that I'm experiencing. Now I'm falling asleep as it's been a very long day – and I know we'll be up early.

(Journal) May 20

Didn't sleep much last night – very warm, and my stomach was yecchhha.

As the time for returning home grows closer, I'm wanting to prolong my travels. I really am frightened. Frightened of having to make decisions as I realize now that never in my life have I had to make any real decisions. Everything has been more or less presented to me. EASY! Palfrey – slowly beginning to gain confidence – wish I had spent more time there – as usual, I never could really understand what Mom and Dad and everyone were trying to tell me. And now I regret lots of things – realizing how difficult I have made it for myself. I'm no closer to making a decision now than I've ever been, but now I'll have to. No more running, drifting… I must settle and seek fulfillment at least now I know that I'm not happy on the road… So very tired of it now…

The Ringo Guest House

For 40 rupees a night we have a decent room. It has a high ceiling, the usual cell-like walls painted a very pale shade of green, a table and chair, mirror and shelves, even hangers in a cupboard. There's an attached toilet, sink, and shower, a fan, and an air cooler (the room's ONLY 35 Rp. if we don't use the cooler – but it does a good job, except for giving me a sore throat and cold)!

After moving in here, we headed for the international students' travels building. We took a taxi to the First National City Bank, filled out forms, waited in a line, waited while the guy filled out a bunch of forms and were told that our bank draft (to be issued to the airline) wouldn't be ready for a couple of hours. So we 3-wheel-rickshawed it back to Connaught Place with the HOT air whipping against our faces. We bought aerogrammes at one point, returned to the travel office where we were brought cokes as it is so hot out today!

Then on to American Express – to check for mail and to send a telex asking the American Express Company in Amsterdam to forward all my mail (and hopefully, the $200) to Paris. But it was after 4:00, so it was closed. We looked at beautiful Rajasthani pieces and I bought a few pouches – one purple one for me; I fell in love with it – embroidered – old – perfect size. I really wanted to buy some over the door decorations – real beauties – but we almost ran out of rupees. The tourist agent owed us 182 rupees – too complicated to explain – I guess we had to pay more which he had to pay back in order for us to get a 10% discount. Then back to the office to sit and wait for over an hour for our plane tickets to be "fetched" from Air France. Yeah! We have our tickets! Friday 1:00 AM to Paris!

(Journal) Wednesday

Tonight is our last night in Delhi – last night in India, last night in the East, last night in a hotel…

I can't believe that finally our trip is coming to an end and that it's time to go home. Now that the time is so close, I'm almost wanting to prolong it – I am frightened! I wish I knew exactly what I am going to be doing when I get home – from what both Gail and Sue say (and everyone else, for that matter), jobs are very difficult to come by. But really, the only thing to do is wait until I get there and things will fall into place, somehow…

Meanwhile – tomorrow night we're flying to Paris! I just can't believe it, that on Thursday morning, we'll be in Paris, France! I'm excited, apprehensive; I mean Paris is the fashion center of the world! And from all I've heard, the Parisians are very cold with their noses up in the air – we shall see – Jerry'll show us a great time, I'm sure…

Today, we woke up at around 9:30 – spaced-out from the mandrax, and headed for American Express where I received letters from Gail and Sue – both of them just returned home from their respective freshman years. They were telling me how boring home was. Belmont certainly will be a drag! Dave changed 30 dollars, and then set off to buy 6 balance scales – I sat and bargained with the ladies selling Rajasthani goods (Gujarati, actually). Anyway, two cops came and arrested the two women for street-vending without a permit. They led them off down the street along with a couple of others, and of course a substantial crowd had gathered. Fifteen minutes later I saw the women – they'd had to baksheesh the pigs 20 rupees each.

Tonight, we ate Indian food on the top floor in the Mohan Singh building, then sugarcane juice (my favorite drink), and then to the Quality for a totally unnecessary ice cream sundae. I really am becoming fat – don't want to go home fat – know I'll eat so much there… must be careful!

Today we bought some Rajasthani pieces, a beautiful embroidered shirt for Dave, one for me, a batiked scarf for Grammy, packed up, and took the 10:30 PM "ex-servicemens' bus" to the airport – Good-bye to Delhi and the East… So we thought…

The airport scene was typically Indian – "queues" to wait in, everyone pushing to the front. So very tired… I fell asleep lying across two chairs…

The Ashoka Hotel, New Delhi

I can't believe that right now it's 3:30 AM and I am sitting at the desk in the most beautiful hotel room I've ever had. Our flight was delayed "indefinitely," so after eating club sandwiches at the airport restaurant, we took a taxi to the Ashoka Hotel, Delhi's number 1 hotel. It's like the Taj Mahal in Bombay; an enclosed city! Restaurants of all sorts, stores, post offices, bank, swimming pool… so plush!

Our room has 2 beds, a night table with telephone for room service (maybe local calls also!), a table and chair, closet with sliding (carved) door, shelves, huge picture window with curtains (of course), really nice carpet, desk with large mirror, 2 lamps, 2 more over each bed, a beautiful bathroom with a tub and even a telephone in the bathroom!

(Journal) Saturday - noon

Yesterday we were here by the pool and apparently missed our flight confirmation – should've flown out last night on Pan Am to Beirut, and changed planes there for Paris. Then we were told that the next flight would be Monday night with Air France. So we had dinner with Bill (met on the flight from Kathmandu). He's the Boeing engineer – quite a life! All expenses paid for at the ritziest places – he's been living at the Ashoka for 4 months working on a contract. Soon he will be flying to Singapore. We went to his suite after dinner, and he has Joni Mitchell's "Blue" album. So good to hear Joni!

After spending a few hours by the pool yesterday, we went into the Samovar to eat. Dave had a delicious shrimp cocktail, and then "chicken in a basket." I had tomato juice, a garden salad, and a cheeseburger. We got a bit carried away with the rich food we were not accustomed to, and I got very sick. I've been mostly vegetarian during the trip, so I imagine eating that burger was simply too much for my system.

Breakfast, brought by room service, was incredible! Cheese and mushroom omelets, Danish pastry, croissant rolls, butter, honey, different preserves, fresh ground coffee, freshly squeezed orange juice…

Also, while sitting in the Rotisserie, we met Thor. He was very drunk – is a steward for SAS – came and sat next to me – kept telling me how much I attracted him – came on very strong…

Today, Dave went to the Air France office – we're on the waiting list for a JAL flight at 7:00 tonight – hope we won't get on and that we'll be able to hang out here until Monday!

(Journal) Monday, May 26 – Ashoka Hotel: Room – 252

Our last night in India (I think!)

India… so very good, yet so very challenging; yes, extreme is the best way of describing this country. This is my last night here and as pleasant as these past few days at the Ashoka have been, I'm very happy to be leaving this screwed-up country with its millions and millions (600,000 people live in 2 square miles of land in Old Delhi!) of people, the majority of whom live such miserable lives that they should be shot and put out of their misery! Floods, droughts, famines, earthquakes – 200 people died of the heat in Bihar a few weeks ago! And in February, many died of exposure when the temperature dropped to 32 degrees F! So very sad; the best solution would be for India to drop her newly acquired atom bomb upon devastated areas such as Bihar…! I can't believe how callous I'm sounding!

And I admit that some pretty lousy things have happened to me; train station scenes to begin with, so many stupid people to deal with… Really, it amazes me how stupid the vast majority of Hindus are. I've met Muslims and Sikhs from Kashmir who are just so much more pleasant to talk to, never mind do business with! Ignorance is one thing, quite tolerable, but stupidity is just too much for me to handle, especially in these quantities! Getting my bag stolen off my lap (while I was wide awake), while riding unreserved from Gorakhpur to Lucknow… what a nightmare!

But some incredibly good things have come my way, also good people. The Shahs' family in Vile Parle – opening their arms to welcome me and Dave into their homes. I have to say upper-class India is astounding. On the whole, that is…

I met many good people in Bombay, Archana being uppermost in my mind. A true Indian beauty. Sixteen years old – already a proper little lady, yet like all others, she is so very naive to the joys (as we see them!) of life. Predestined to go to college, in the meantime learning to sew, embroider, cook – preparing to make some Indian man, chosen by her parents, a perfect wife. She's so sincere! So sweet… caring for me so much, for the spice I've brought into her simple life.

And Goa was beautiful and mellow; the people smiling and saying hello; not always approaching with, "From which country are you coming from?" or, "What is your purpose for coming to India?" Too bad I got sick in Goa after having that terrible sunburn on my chest… somehow, it's difficult to have fond memories of any place in which you were sick or got robbed. I really should've returned to Agra – somehow I didn't get as high on the Taj Mahal as I should have – it was right after my bag was stolen – I was still sick over having lost my other diary… but still I must admit that there couldn't be any building more beautiful, more perfect on the face of this earth.

So much to learn in India! So many customs; so much pageantry… I feel that my trips to India have been very valuable – I've learned so much about this crazy world!

Finally we have flight confirmations for tonight's flight to Paris; #191 – departs New Delhi at 1:50 AM, but this morning we were told it was already running 1/2 hour behind schedule.

We haven't yet settled our bill – luckily Dave had the foresight to check with the reception desk, and sure enough, a voucher had been issued for the first day only! So they called Air France and supposedly straightened things out – we won't feel secure until 9:30, when all gets taken care of.

In the meantime, it's been a very relaxing few days – lounging by the pool, tanning myself (pretty brown now!), swimming in a really magnificent pool! Eating, eating – gaining weight – yesterday we had two incredible meals – to the "Peacock" for their 30 Rp. buffet luncheon – so much delicious food! Cold turkey slices, fish, all sorts of salads, pickled things, curries, dal, Jell-O molds, fruit, custard things, delicious sweets…

For a late dinner we went to The Supper Club which is incredibly plush! Started off with grasshoppers and soup – French onion, creme du tomate. I had "coq du vin" – chicken cooked in red wine with large mushrooms, button onions, carrots, spinach – so delicious! Espresso for dessert! We went and sat with an English couple, who had come especially to see the Indian dancing. Throughout our dinner a bard was playing – popular music – appealing to all – not great; playing a variation of 50's jazz and current rock.

Then the most incredible woman danced – to the sound of the harmonium, and a woman singing as only Indians can sing – so high and nasal… The dancer wore a very sparkly dress – bells around her ankles – so flowing – expressive – she really can move her body into amazing positions – so graceful, and together with the music!

No hassle when we settled our bill – I can't believe how much money we spent – I must admit that I've fully enjoyed laying back for these past four days… swimming. Too bad I'll most likely lose my tan before I get home…

Bon Voyage… we're off to Paris in 15 hours. I won't believe it until I get there and then we'll have to deal with the culture shock – very difficult to imagine.

CHAPTER SEVENTEEN

HOME TO BELMONT

EUROPE

(Journal) Wednesday, May 28 – 9:30 am in Paris!

Our flight took off at around 3:00 pm. Air France offers lousy service and lousy food. Stopped over in Abu Dhabi, a barren desert wasteland, and then in Istanbul, where we were able to step out and take a look at the duty free shops. I would've loved to buy a backgammon board for Sue, but there weren't any under $50.

Of course we didn't get any sleep on the plane. Landed in Paris, Charles De Gaulle airport at around noon. As soon as we stepped off the plane, we heard Dave's name over a speaker, saying there was a message for him. Yeah! Jerry gave us directions to his house, telling us to leave our packs at the Maillot terminal. However, he neglected to tell us to take the metro to Passy and then walk to Rue Gavaruin. We figured Gavaruin was near Maillot, and the info desk told us it was a 10-minute walk. We found what we thought was 11 Rue Garvarni, but turned out to be Galvani – instead of Paris 16, it was Paris 17. A really nice French woman tried to help us. Language was a problem; Hindi and English and French are one big jumble in

my mind. An incredibly jolly nice Frenchman took us in his Renault to the metro, where we could take #6 ligne and get out at Passy, and then walk.

Such a tremendous city! Cafes everywhere to be seen; stores of all sorts; yes, people really do dress to kill here. I feel pretty strange – all moves so fast and everything's so large! Driving along – the rain pouring down – typical European weather… and suddenly, in front of us we saw the incredible Arc de Triomphe in all its splendor! Paris! Full of culture – so many things to do and see here!

We took the metro; really nice subway system; so clean and efficient – a pleasure! And easy to get around the city. After asking a bunch of people, we found Jerry's apartment, and the door was opened by his 80 yr. old Aunt (whose health is poor). Also, she's a bit senile… She began speaking in Armenian to David. Together with the little French we know, we managed to communicate quite well. The apartment is amazing – Jerry really has traveled extensively and has so many things! Collections of every kind: boxes, pipes, glass eggs, ash trays, match boxes, even sugar cubes! All is arranged beautifully! His room (mine for the time being – he and Dave are sharing the fold-out couch in the living room).

How could I have forgotten to mention customs! We claimed our baggage and headed for customs. We put our packs on the counter, the guy looked at our passports and said, "O.K., finished." We couldn't believe that was all… We walked through, and a young guy in a velvet jacket flashed a badge, asked us where we were coming from. "Delhi." How long had we been in India? Had we been in Nepal? "Yes." We had to follow him to a hidden room, where after the French couple and their 2 kids were issued out – the mother very shaken – told me that everything was looked at – sure enough the bastards went through every bit of our things – even began cutting up and chemically testing our halazone tablets. Gave Dave some grief about the pipe he brought for Jerry – made me step out of the room and searched David – sticking things into his shoes, etc. – never have I been made more nervous, and we were perfectly clean! Really, not even an apology. So humiliating!!!

Now we're off to American Express and then to begin our round of sight-seeing. The Eiffel Tower, etc.

(Journal) May 29

Yesterday was a good day. On the way to the metro, we walked by the Eiffel Tower – Jerry's apt. sure is centrally located! The Eiffel Tower is all as impressive as I thought, even more so.

Fountains in the park below… but so many tourists, it's amazing. I guess the tourist season has begun… Met a black American from Calif. – Liviticus – children of God; they really are everywhere! He asked me to say hello to "Brother Aaron" if I happen to meet him in or around Boston. American Express is really big! Three stories, including gift shops, etc. There was no mail for either of us, but sent a telex to Amsterdam and the money should be here today. And mail in a day or two.

Oh! Happy news – yesterday morning Dave received a telegram from Vahan – everything's okay at home – his mother's out of the hospital… so Dave'll be coming to Zurich. Such a relief!

While I was waiting in line to send the telex, we met Sonny (Israel Rosen) from San Francisco. It really is a small world! He's lived with Bruce for the past two years! The three of us sat around drinking beer (me with my lemonade), and Sonny called home asking for money (yesterday was his birthday)… Then we all went to "Le printemps" to meet Jerry; Printemps is a department store like Lord and Taylors or Sak's… Jerry's job is to "help tourists spend their money" by translating for them. We all went to lunch – first up to the top floor of "Printemps" – really nice restaurant – delicious-looking food; incredible variety, but Jerry changed his mind, so down we went to look for good sandwiches – in a deli and out again – finally sat outside at a café. Typical French bread with ham and cheese, so much for not eating meat… I have eaten lots of chicken lately, and I must say I enjoy it! After lunch, we headed in the direction of the Rodin Museum, but didn't make it past the Eiffel Tower; we just sat by a little park full of children riding go-carts. We wrote a joint letter to Bruce and Joanne, not explaining where or how we met up with Sonny.

Then we headed back to meet Jerry, as we'd decided to go and see *Tommy* – incredible movie! I'm glad I understand the story now, incredibly heavy! The movie was very well done; but as it is typical of The Who it was so loud!

Afterwards, we went to Champs Elysees – incredible! But not at all my kind of place... a wide boulevard with hundreds of restaurants, bars, boutiques, clubs. Everyone in Paris dresses to kill – makes me feel like such a slob in my jeans.

Today it's really lousy out – typical Paris – cold and raining, whereas yesterday was a gorgeous sunny day! We're planning on going to Am. Express to meet Sonny and to hopefully receive the money. Then I want to go to the post office and telephone Grammy – that'll

make her really happy I know! Costs 38 francs for three minutes! Expensive, but okay, considering I've been away so long and haven't called at all. Since it's raining, we'll probably go to Le Louvre! Or to some other museum.

Today we left the apt. at around 11:00, walked to Trocadero (near the Eiffel Tower) to catch the metro into Havre – Gumartin, where American Express and Printemps are located. No money. Then we went to the Post Office, and I called Grammy. At first the operator told me there'd be a 15-minute delay, but after only 3 minutes, I was called – caught totally off-guard – and suddenly I heard Grammy's voice as though she were next door. It was strange; unfortunately, my emotions got the better of me... and I couldn't help crying.

I managed to tell Grammy that we'll be taking the train to Zurich on either Tuesday or Wednesday, spending a week or so there, and then flying to Montreal. Grammy'll be going to California on June 12 – maybe I'll get back in time to see her off... I doubt it, though.

We went to Notre Dame – spectacular! So far I haven't been in the least bit disappointed – Paris is truly beautiful. So many old buildings – incredible architecture. So ornate, romantic... I really am amazed by the numbers of tourists, especially Americans, in Paris. After walking all around and in Notre Dame and sitting in the garden behind, we stopped at a sidewalk cafe, and Dave had a sandwich. I wish I could eat and eat and never get fat. The pastries everywhere are amazing, and the sandwiches... We went looking all over for a salad for me, but couldn't find one. Oh well, does me good not to eat. Besides, tonight Jerry's aunt is cooking dinner: steak, chicken, asparagus – poor woman really is sickly… spends most of her days in bed. The doctor says she should be in the hospital, but she refuses. Actually, staying at home is probably best for her. As Mom has always said, it's the end when an elderly person goes into the hospital.

(Journal) Friday, May 30

Today we visited Le Louvre! Never have I been so enthralled… so vast! We headed straight for the Mona Lisa – ahhh – truly, the most gorgeous painting I've ever seen – completely captured me – her eyes following me around – her mouth smiling at me – her hands so beautifully expressive – the colors so lifelike – subdued. I even paid a franc to listen to the history over an earphone. We walked and walked, so much to see! We managed to see (barely) over 1/2 of the museum although we didn't spend much time by any one picture, except for the Mona Lisa, of course. Unfortunately, the Michelangelo galleries were closed, but we're planning to return another day. We saw the ancient Egyptian, Roman, and Greek sculptures… Some of it is so very old!

The Louvre itself is such an amazing structure – so majestic; full of archways – carved marble doorways – and the ceilings full of paintings… so ornate! All of the rooms have tremendous windows or glass ceilings, allowing natural light to pervade the entire building, showing each and every piece of art as it was meant to be seen.

I can't get over how beautiful this city is! There's an endless number of things to do and places to visit. Tomorrow we'll try to make it to the Rodin Museum. It's free in the mornings for students, and we only had to pay 1/2 price at the Louvre (2.50 francs, instead of 5).

Loneliness really is all over… I feel so sad for Jerry. He's so sincerely kind, so generous, so loving, yet he's so alone – has no friends in Paris – sure, many acquaintances – but there certainly is a difference. I know that from my own experiences…

Anyway – now that his aunt is so sick, he's faced with the fact that soon he shall be alone. For so many years, he's lived with his aunt (both his parents were killed by the Russians although I don't know when). She was talking to me this afternoon. We actually managed to communicate well. My French isn't so bad, and I find that I can understand a lot more than I thought. She was asking me why Jerry doesn't get married, pointing out that Dave has me and vice versa, but when she dies, he'll be alone.

Tonight we talked and talked. Jerry is tired of France and the cold French people – although he's lived here for 20 years, somehow he hasn't found any friends… His aunt wants him to get married – and I know even Jerry would like to – he was talking about it tonight, asking me why I don't want to be married, saying that when he was 19 he said the same thing. Now he's 42 – where did it get him…

He's wanting to move to either Brazil or to the States. We're trying to tell him that it won't work for him to fly somewhere and expect to step right into a niche – job, home, etc. – that he should take advantage of all the names and addresses in the US and write to people and ask if any of them know of any jobs. Jerry says he's too proud. He just has never known real friendship – or very seldomly – he cares for Dave so much – it will be difficult saying good-bye… Again he's been giving us so many things! A pair of boots for Dave – every day he brings home perfumes – a tortoise shell bangle today. Enough for now – time for sleeping!

(Journal) May 31

Very tired – just returned from St. Germain – so many people out drinking beer or coffee. Somehow it seems as though the majority of French people aren't happy, or at least, that they lead very boring lives… Jerry always says how cold and unfriendly and selfish the French are. Never will a Frenchman invite you to his home… Instead he'll invite you for a beer at the corner bar…

This morning I went to American Express to find $400 waiting for me! Mom sent it again as I asked, but also, it WAS in Amsterdam… no problem – I'll just bring them home $200.

We went to the Madeleine Cathedral – truly beautiful – so ornate – just sat peacefully for about half an hour. Met Jerry for lunch at 2:00. He gets a 15% discount at Printemps, so he showed me some things that were on sale. Unfortunately, nothing looked well. Prices are so ridiculously high! Maybe more will be on sale Monday.

(Journal) Monday, June 2

Yesterday we took the train to Versailles. Such a nice sun-shining day! We walked around the Palace – very impressive size; so ornate, but the paintings and even the sculptures were not of fine quality. We walked and walked in the gardens by the houses of Marie-Antoinette; so beautifully green – lots of flowers – rhododendrons of all colors… A nice day… and from the train station, Jerry called his friend Michael, and we were all invited for dinner! Michael, his wife Miret, and their 3 yr. old daughter Virginia live in a beautiful modern house not far from Versailles. The French countryside is so picturesque!

There were ten people (or so) at the house – really lively atmosphere. Miret's mother is here for a month – lives in Houston, Texas – owns a French restaurant there. I am amazed at how pretty she is – looks so young! Keeps herself very well. Cocktails (margaritas) were served, and French bread with a spread made of a meat mixture, pickles, cheese, and salami. Later, baked potatoes wrapped in tinfoil and baked directly in the fire were served with sour cream.

Such crazy nice people! Jerry met them on Ibiza a few years ago – an island off the coast of Spain! At around 11:45 we were asked if we wished to spend the night; as today also was a day off for Jerry, there was no reason not to! Miret even had to go out (to Michael's mother's) to borrow blankets!

For breakfast we had pancakes with boysenberry jam… Michael went to work (real estate), but returned at around 11:30, and we went for a ride to see "typical French countryside." So nice! Rolling, green hillsides – castles all around! We went to three – just walked around – taking pictures and gathering flowers (I have so many now!) – then we stopped in a typically French village – saw a typically French graveyard – and drank wine (I had Canada Dry ginger ale) at a tiny pub. Next door was a bakery. We bought bread and pastry for lunch. Saw more of the country. The villages are so quaint.

Someday I'd like to spend time in this country, learn the language although I feel that with a little practice, it'll come fairly easily, as I did pretty well (Je pense!), especially with Virginia.

Such great people! Jerry goes there every weekend – I can see why! They're crazy.

(Journal) June 3 - Dave's birthday

Last night I felt lousy – had the shits worse than ever in the East! Guess the rich French food got to me… This morning we packed everything up, washed some clothes and ourselves, and then headed into town. Unfortunately, all museums are closed on Tuesdays – a shame considering we were at Michael and Miret's yesterday and tomorrow's our last day. Anyway, we went in to meet Jerry for lunch – before which we bought our train tickets on the 6th floor of "Le Printemps" – so nice to only have to spend 5 minutes instead of 5 days of hassling!

After lunch at the store's canteen (the employees get a really good deal – hot lunch is very inexpensive), we looked around the store. With Jerry's 15% discount it really is a shame that I couldn't find a nice skirt cheap enough to buy… I bought only a nice wooden cork screw for dad.

Finally, at around 4:00 PM we headed for Sacre Coeur – so picturesque the way it's set upon a hill. A man was feeding the birds. He had a plastic bag filled with food, and he'd hold his hand up and so many sparrows ate from his hand! I held up the remainder of Dave's stale ice cream cone, but the birds certainly weren't interested. The man beckoned for me to go down the steps and join him. He then took the cone, threw it on the ground and handed me some of the dough or whatever he had, and all the birds came to me – such an incredible feeling! Sparrows are adorable…

Only bummer of the day… Jerry had given Dave a really nice blazer made from denim. We were sitting feeding the birds, and Dave took a picture of me (Mom will love it!) – afterwards we got up and climbed the many stairs to the church; we sat in peace for 10-15 minutes or so and when we got up we realized we didn't have Dave's jacket – we looked in vain, but gave up after half an hour… easy come, easy go – but it's too bad, because out of the many things Jerry's given Dave, that jacket was his favorite.

Been thinking lots lately about what I'll do when I get home. A yoga course is a definite for the summer. Friends World is #1 at the moment, as my interests are so varied. I'd like to get back into some music, learn French – before I lose everything I've learned – and I'd like to work with children. Plus, I wish to join some sort of a writing workshop. I do so enjoy writing and in general relating my thoughts and experiences to others.

I'm planning to recapture as much of my diary as is possible – by reading over and copying my letters, which Dad has kept for me; there's plenty of room in this book…

And now it's time for sleeping. We had a delicious meal: chicken, peas and carrots, mushrooms and scallions, fried in butter, champagne, and a cherry tart with ice cream, cake, and raisin rum!

(Journal) June 4

It's 11:30 PM and we're on the way to Zurich! Got up this morning and headed for Le Louvre. Such a beautiful sun-shining day! We went to see the "Michel-Ange" exhibit – were surprised to find only two sculptures – both entitled, "Les esclaves." There was a slide show (in French only). Very beautiful. Someday I hope to get to Florence and see "David," etc. We walked around for a while – saw the crown jewels – Napoleon's crown, tremendous jewels – diamond 2" in diameter.

We walked to Printemps via Avenue de L'Opera – didn't realize how close it is! Met Jerry for lunch, and again we went to the employees' canteen.

Finally we made it to Musee Rodin – wish I knew there was such a nice garden there – would've been nice to have a picnic.

Jerry was very tense tonight. I feel really sorry for him. He asked us why we weren't going to stay longer in Paris, what were we going to do in Europe. He admitted that he was jealous… he wanted to take the train and meet us in Zurich on Sunday morning…

(Journal) June 5

The train was exactly on time, arriving in Zurich at 7:19 AM. Although we had plenty of room to stretch out and sleep (there were only 3 of us in a cabin for 6 and the seats push together), I only slept for a couple of hours. Mike from L.A. shared the cabin…

We called Margaret and Nils (waking them up), and Nils came to pick us up in their blue VW van.

Zurich is every bit as clean as we'd expected – very new and shiny looking… Blue and white trains speeding all over… everyone speaking Swiss and German – feels pretty mellow! But oh so expensive – we changed $20 – 2.49 francs per dollar. Coffee is about 1.50 francs per cup!!

Wonderful to be with Margaret and Nils again – such good, good friends – can't think of better… and their apartment (flat) is the nicest I've been in – 3 rooms plus kitchen and bathrooms (no shower, but downstairs there's a really nice one so no problem). The living room where we're all sitting now is so warm – a good stereo system – this chair I'm now sitting in is so incredibly comfortable – and rocks… Margaret made a cover for it out of scraps from old trousers – triangular pieces of corduroy – plus, there are two "ploppy seats" – material stuffed with bits of styrofoam – very comfy. Lots of nice pictures on the walls, amazing taste!

Unfortunately, they're unable to find work – they make scale models of buildings for architects, but the Swiss govt. put a freeze on building, as there are already too many flats, too expensive

for people to rent! So Margaret is doing office work in the mornings for the time being.

Today, after we unpacked and made a mess – we drove to their "workshop" – intricate machines! And then walked around Zurich a bit beginning by the large lake. It's so nice and clean also! We walked down side streets. We found a nice flea market – many freaks selling handmade and eastern goods at pretty reasonable prices. After stopping for a beer (ice cream for Margaret and I), we headed on to see one of the incredible models Margaret made (earlier, we'd looked at lots of photos of models they've made – the one we saw was made entirely of wood and was an entire village). We stopped at a pet shop to look at the tremendous hairy spiders in the window and went in to see the birds – a beautiful 2 foot red parrot-like bird on a perch – and two fairly small black birds kept saying, "ciao" – and one said, "Buenos Noches," and a few other things in Spanish – and some in Swiss German asked Nils if he had a pain in his head! It totally flipped us all out!

We booked our plane tickets! Flying to Montreal a week from Monday night. I'll be in Belmont at home in 9 days. Really tough to imagine what it'll be like… Anxious but not so anxious to get there – not going to be so easy… time to make decisions.

(Journal) June 6

Ahhhh – the Swiss Alps. Sitting high on a hillside. All around is green and fresh and huge mountains covered with snow jutting up – so white against the blue sky – the rolling green hills all around. Never have I seen so many wild flowers! Everywhere – fields of pink, purple, yellow, white, red all together and so lushly green! Brown houses – quaint

This time of day is my favorite with everything looking golden. We're just outside of the village "Grindelwald" – 150 miles from Zurich

– we drove through Zurich and "Interlochen" – a little village "locked" in the mountains by two large lakes. Switzerland is truly beautiful! Fairyland!

The Eiger! 3970 meters – with a 3500 ft. steep sheer face – many a climber has died on that mountain.

Margaret has a lot to teach. Because she grew up in the mountains, she knows about all the plants and wild flowers. She shows me which flowers to eat and which are good for making tea. How little I really know! When I am home I have so much learning to do, but it will be more structured, demanding more self-discipline than I've had to employ in a long time. For now I can enjoy being here in this magnificent valley. Pretty soon Margaret will be cooking up a cheese fondue, and the sun will set over the mountains.

(Journal) Sunday, June 8

This long weekend has been great! Clear and sunny the whole time... stopping in the lovely city of Bern on our way to Grindelwald and seeing big brown bears – just like teddy bears! Walking on their hind legs and dancing so people will throw food to them...

It really is nice to own a van – so easy to travel! A mobile home... maybe some day. But first things first! Now I have to think about going home to Belmont. It's hard to know exactly what I'll do there. So many things to choose from! Literally the whole world...

Today, we drove up to a pass – not so very high – but with beautiful views of the mountains. We climbed up and up through the beautiful woods, trying to get a better view, but couldn't find a clearing! My favorite type of hiking (climbing involving exertion) is definitely through woods without a trail.

(Journal) June 9

Stayed around the apartment today – reading an Agatha Christie mystery (enjoyed it!) – went shopping for food with Margaret, came home and baked butterscotch brownies – really good, but different – it was fun converting to the metric system! Used hazelnuts, really good.

So many people to see – it will be happy, but strange – maybe disillusioning – although I really don't think I have too many illusions

– just one big question mark! I just have no idea what to expect at all! From people, places, things – Linda K. wrote that I may not recognize parts of Cambridge and Boston, as so many renovations are happening in preparation for the bicentennial. Many things are different at home – new furniture in the living room – a shower in our bathroom… the yard will have more of a vegetable garden…

Aaahhhhhhh! I must be strong – hold my head high – so many reunions to look forward to! Mom and Dad – Debbie, Jeri – Kitty (who will probably be totally apathetic, maybe a bit annoyed that he'll have to share my bed with me! Mom writes that he always sleeps there…), and Sue, Linda K., Gail (wonder how long she will be in Florida?!) – and when I'll see Nancy – and what will it be like seeing everyone… Linda T. is home also – Jeanne.

Emily and other Palfrey-ites – Ned! Caroline! Carde! So many friends to see! So many things to do – hassles, decisions, dentist! Doctor – complete physical is in line! Will I go job hunting right away? It's hard to imagine waitressing again. Although the money was good, I don't think I could handle going back to Charlie's Beef and Beer. Helen would be too heavy. I don't want to work so many nights, too screwy for my system!

(Journal) Tuesday, June 10

In 48 hours, we'll be in Montreal. We confirmed flight reservations for Thursday – Vaughan will meet us there. I'm beginning to freak a little… what will it be like?!?! I have so many people to see it's almost ridiculous – I should start an appointment book!

I just can't stop thinking about everyone and everything at home, how I've drifted away… Who will I be close with and who will – or has already – drifted away? I'm sad that Cedric left for Alaska – I miss him – and I feel bad that he and Dave have seen so little of one another – too bad they didn't head west together.

Yes, lots of people will be watching me when I get home… wondering – asking questions – I have a feeling that Mom and Dad will be fantastic – they actually always have been – hopefully I'll be able to appreciate them more… without taking my frustration out on them.

I may have changed a lot during the past 8 months, but somehow I still lose my temper too often – not understanding why, but unable to control myself, a terrible fault! I must concentrate.

Tonight, after supper (hot dogs, mashed potatoes, and carrots), we drove out (40 minutes or so) into the country to a farm. When Margaret and Nils were traveling, a couple lived in their flat. She's Swiss, and he's half Swiss, half Canadian. They moved to this farm where they live with 2 other couples. We went there for the purpose of picking up Margaret's two birds.

A beautiful farmhouse – very big – old, but a great kitchen and bathroom. Sheep, a horse, pigs, chickens, cats, dogs, ducks, geese, many rabbits! They breed them for eating and for selling. The "Big Daddy" rabbit is the biggest rabbit I've ever seen! At least 2 ft. long – a 6" in diameter head – incredible! Really beautiful – licked my fingers…

Yes, those people really are together – but I should keep in mind the fact that they are 10 years older than I am. Tomorrow is the last day of our incredible journey…

(Journal) Thursday, June 12

Saying good-bye is always so difficult! Especially when it's to two beautiful friends and I don't know when I'll see them again…

Here we are at the airport – same terminal as we were in when we flew from here to Munich – but this time we're going home!!! Eight months certainly did fly by!

I'M HOME!!! It feels so good… The flight was pleasant – landed in Montreal at around 4:00 (Montreal time) – picked up our packs and headed towards customs – but the next thing we knew we were outside the terminal and there were Vahan and Paul Sarkesian – no customs!

In the plane, sitting next to us was a couple who live in an Ashram in Poona – really nice people. I remember seeing them at the Bombay Amer. Express office! We made a beautiful trade: one of my little bone boxes for an incredible pouch – old Chinese brocade! Plus, she gave me a vial of sandalwood oil…

Rainy and cold out – but 'twas a very comfortable journey in Vaughan's 1964 Caddy. We stopped at McDonald's – mmmm! I have to admit that tasted good!

US customs were pretty thorough – but at least the officials were pleasant! I didn't mind at all! I called home from White River Junction (VT-NH border) – everyone got on the phone, and 2 and a half hours later (1:15 AM) I reached home – There really is no place like home!

Standing on the front lawn with the rain pouring down upon us, hugging Daddy, feeling so secure, so safe, crying uncontrollably… And Mom, we just held one another, both sobbing. Followed her into their beautiful living room and there was the chess set I sent sitting majestically upon the board Deb found, atop the incredible antique table Mom and Dad found, and the Tibetan carpet looks gorgeous by the fireplace. And Debbie… so silent, emotions working in her face – somehow there seems to be a barrier which I wish to overcome!

And then running upstairs to wake up Jeri, into her darkened room, softly saying her name and hearing, "Karen?" – pulling her out of bed and hugging – my god – she's grown so much! At least 4 inches.

Aaahhhh… There's no place like home.

EPILOGUE

TODAY

Though I have yet to return to Nepal, that trip left an indelible imprint on my life. Even now, forty-four years later, I find myself being reminded of something that happened during those powerful eight months on just about a daily basis. A smell of champa incense, a "Made in Nepal" label, prayer flags in front of a store, a curry dish on a menu, chai available in every coffee house…

I'm grateful to have been to that part of the world during a time when life was simpler. The Russians had not yet invaded Afghanistan, Nepal hadn't had any devastating earthquakes, Kathmandu Valley was pristine so unlike the horrific pollution that pervades the area now. Rather than the hotels which I hear dot the Himalayan landscape, we'd stay in people's homes alongside Nepalese families. Terrorism was not yet at the top of the daily news…

And for just a bit of perspective, Dave and I spent a total of $4200.00 including all flights and overland travel expenses. Our round trip ticket from Montreal to Munich was $304.00 so long as we used it within a year. We chose to return home from Zurich rather than Munich, and because it's closer to Boston we actually got $4.00 back.

Karen Solomon is a speaker, coach, image consultant, author and adventure seeker. All her life's work inspires others to find the adventures in their lives and encourage them to play a "big game."

She is the author of *Sexy, Sassy & Starting Over: Recipes for a Sweet & Savory Life After Divorce* and lives in San Diego, California. Her website is www.KarenSolomon.com.

www.ingramcontent.com/pod-product-compliance
Lightning Source LLC
Chambersburg PA
CBHW040000080526
44586CB00027B/2822